SUPERINTENDENT LEADERSHIP

"For Review Only"

To my precious family:
My husband Greg Wilmore,
and our beloved children
Brandon Greggory Wilmore
Brooke Elaine Wilmore
Brittani Leigh Wilmore Rollen
J. Ryan Rollen

I love you from the deepest parts of my heart.

"Write the vision and make it plain on tablets that he may run who reads it.
For the vision is yet for an appointed time;
But at the end it will speak, and it will not lie.
Though it tarries, wait for it because it will surely come."

Habakkuk 2:2–3
New King James Version

SUPERINTENDENT LEADERSHIP

APPLYING
THE
EDUCATIONAL
LEADERSHIP
CONSTITUENT
COUNCIL
(ELCC)
STANDARDS
FOR
IMPROVED
DISTRICT
PERFORMANCE

ELAINE L. WILMORE

CORWIN PRESS
A SAGE Company
Thousand Oaks, CA 91320

For information:

Corwin Press
A SAGE Company
2455 Teller Road
Thousand Oaks, California 91320
www.corwinpress.com

SAGE Ltd.
1 Oliver's Yard
55 City Road
London EC1Y 1SP
United Kingdom

SAGE India Pvt. Ltd.
B 1/I 1 Mohan Cooperative
  Industrial Area
Mathura Road, New Delhi 110 044
India

SAGE Asia-Pacific Pte. Ltd.
33 Pekin Street #02-01
Far East Square
Singapore 048763

Printed in the United States of America.

Library of Congress Cataloging-in-Publication Data

Wilmore, Elaine L.
Superintendent leadership: applying the educational leadership constituent council standards for improved district performance/Elaine L. Wilmore.
    p. cm.
Includes bibliographical references and index.
ISBN 978-1-4129-5540-9 (cloth)
ISBN 978-1-4129-5541-6 (pbk.)
    1. School superintendents—In-service training—Standards—United States.
2. School management and organization—United States. 3. Educational leadership—United States. I. Title.

LB2831.72.W55 2008
371.2′011—dc22   2007042623

This book is printed on acid-free paper.

08   09   10   11   12   10   9   8   7   6   5   4   3   2   1

Acquisitions Editor:	Hudson Perigo
Editorial Assistant:	Lesley Blake
Production Editor:	Eric Garner
Copy Editor:	Paula L. Fleming
Typesetter:	C&M Digitals (P) Ltd.
Proofreader:	Charlotte J. Waisner
Indexer:	Molly Hall
Cover Designer:	Michael Dubowe
Graphic Designer:	Lisa Riley

Contents

Preface

The focus of *Superintendent Leadership: Applying the Educational Leadership Constituent Council Standards for Improved District Performance* is the critical importance of the superintendent in creating, nurturing, and sustaining a climate that values the soul of the school district within its political, social, economic, legal, and cultural context. Although a myriad of books exists on school leadership, climate, and change, none addresses the issues from the standpoint of the superintendent as steward of the school's vision. *Superintendent Leadership* deals with these issues from the perspective of the school district as central to the essence of a learning community.

Superintendent Leadership is both unique in format and timely. The separate administrative standards of the National Council for the Accreditation of Teacher Education (NCATE) and the Interstate School Leaders Licensure Consortium (ISLLC) have merged into one set of agreed-upon standards for the development of future superintendents and the professional development of existing ones. These are called the Educational Leadership Constituent Council (ELCC) standards and are the basis upon which this book is written. This consequently makes *Superintendent Leadership: Applying the Educational Leadership Constituent Council Standards for Improved District Performance* both distinctive and opportune in its approach of tying the new standards to practical yet research-based application for superintendents and others interested in school leadership within the learning community. Although based upon eminent leadership and management theory and research, the book is written in an informative yet practical, readable, interesting, insightful, and inspiring manner. Future administrators may use it as a text in university coursework in school leadership. Current administrators may use it for individual or group reflective professional development.

Superintendent Leadership is written in accordance with the established validated research base established by the National Council for the Accreditation of Teacher Education, the Interstate School Leaders

Licensure Consortium, the National Policy Board for Educational Administration, the American Association of School Administrators, the National Association of Secondary School Superintendents, and the National Association for Elementary School Superintendents. For years, each group has had its own set of standards for the superintendent. Only now have they agreed upon the common set of ELCC standards that are addressed here.

Superintendent Leadership provides both a global philosophy of school leadership as provided in the ELCC standards as well as targeted, specific treatment of the components within each standard. This is done through discussion, examples, problem-based learning, an assessment model, and reflective questions and activities for individuals or groups engaged in professional development opportunities. Case studies based on the experiences of the author and others are included for each standard. The scenarios are designed to help the reader take the theory of the standards and apply it in practical reality. However, all names, schools, and districts have been changed. The book is equally appropriate for preservice superintendents as well as current superintendents, assistant superintendents, deans of instruction, instructional supervisors, and others interested in the development and nurturance of the learning community.

Acknowledgments

Of everything in my books, the acknowledgments are always the hardest to write. I have so many wonderful friends and colleagues who love and support me that I am way beyond blessed. As always, my best blessings are my family members: my husband Greg, our precious children Brandon, Brooke, Brittani, and her wonderful husband Ryan. I am also blessed with great friends who pick me up, make me laugh, and nurture me when I least deserve it. These must always include Helen and Wes Nelson; Dr. Joe and Kathy Martin; JoNell and Larry Jones; Dr. Wade, Renea, and Emily Smith; Dr. Bob and Becky Shaw; Rev. Bob and JoAnn Graham; Dr. Linda and Ron Townzen; Paula and Gary Moresco; Wanda and John Rollen; Donna and Milton Walker; Billie Westbrook; and Kee Badders. Kudos also must go to both the Texas Council of Professors of Educational Administration and the National Council of Professors of Educational Administration, both of which I was honored and privileged to serve as president. Last, mega-mega-kudos to Honor Fede and the Educational Leadership Constituent Council, without whom none of this would be possible.

God bless you all, and *thank you for loving me!*

—*Elaine*

Corwin Press gratefully acknowledges the contributions of the following people:

Randel Beaver
Superintendent
Archer City ISD
Archer City, TX

Marie Blum
Superintendent
Canaseraga Central School District
Canaseraga, NY

Dr. Vicki Denmark
Area Superintendent
Fulton County Schools
Atlanta, GA

Janie P. Edmonds, EdD
Superintendent of Schools
Mendham, NJ

Mike Ford
Superintendent of Schools
Phelps-Clifton Springs Central School
District
Clifton Springs, NY

Robert A. Frick, EdD
Superintendent of Schools
Lampeter-Strasburg School District
Lampeter, PA

Douglas Gordon Hesbol
Superintendent
Laraway CCSD 70C
Joliet, IL

Dan Lawson
Superintendent
Tullahoma City Schools
Tullahoma, TN

Kathy Malnar, EdD
Superintendent
Hudson Area Schools
Hudson, MI

Rick Miller, PhD
Superintendent
Oxnard School District
Oxnard, CA

Kenneth Morseon
Superintendent
Cleary School for the Deaf
Nesconset, NY

Janie L. Nusser
Superintendent
South Seneca Central School District
Interlaken, NY

About the Author

 **Elaine L. Wilmore**, PhD, is the assistant vice president for educational networking and director of educational leadership at Dallas Baptist University in Texas. A prolific writer, she is the author of four other leadership books and multiple chapters in books as well as numerous published articles and poems. Wilmore is also "writer-in-residence" at the historic Ingleside Bed and Breakfast in Brenham, Texas. She has formerly served as special assistant to the dean for NCATE Accreditation and Associate Professor of Educational Leadership and Policy Studies at the University of Texas at Arlington (UTA), president of the National Council of Professors of Educational Administration, president of the Texas Council of Professors of Educational Leadership, and president of the Board of Trustees of the Cleburne Independent School District. She is the founding director of School Administration Programs, Educational Leadership UTA, and the Scholars of Practice Program at UTA, where she was principal investigator for multiple grants for innovative field-based principal preparation programs. She has served as chair of educational administration and director of university program development at UTA, where she also developed and was the original chair of the faculty governance committee for the College of Education.

Dr. Wilmore is, and has been, active on many local, state, and national boards. These include serving on the executive committee of the National Council of Professors of Educational Administration, the American Educational Research Association Executive Committee on the Teaching in Educational Administration SIG, the Texas Principals Leadership Initiative, the Texas Consortium of Colleges of Teacher Education, the Cleburne Public Library Advisory Board, the Advisory Board for the Museum of Glass Made in America, and she has served as a program/folio reviewer for the Educational Leadership Constituent Council. She holds the distinction of being among the very few who have served, or are currently serving, as both a private school and public school district board of trustees member.

Dr. Wilmore served as a former public school teacher, counselor, and elementary and middle school principal before moving to higher education. In addition to her significant work in educational leadership and innovative program development, she enjoys reading, writing, walking, music, spending time with those she loves, and anything chocolate. She is married and the mother of three wonderful children, Brandon Greggory Wilmore, Brooke Elaine Wilmore, Brittani Leigh Wilmore Rollen, a fabulous son-in-law, Ryan Rollen, and two outstanding Pugs named Lacianna "Lacie" and Annabella Rose. She greatly misses her parents, Lee and Irene Litchfield, who are in Heaven, and seeks to honor their memory through the way she lives her life each day.

The Educational Leadership Constituent Council Standards as Tools for Improved District Performance

"The most beautiful stones have been tossed by the wind, washed by the waters, and polished to brilliance by life's strongest storms."

—Anonymous

SUPERINTENDENT CONCERNS GENERATED BY A CHANGING SOCIETY

The superintendent is the CEO of the school system in its entirety. It is the position that oversees all facets of the district, from personnel to academics to finance to community involvement. The role of today's superintendent has changed considerably in recent years (Berman, 2005). The dynamics of society as they relate to schools have resulted in the superintendent, as the voice and face of "established education," often coming under fire (Hoyle, 2004). Today's superintendents must deal with internal and external political and governance issues that have arisen due to societal changes. These issues, among others, have generated a new breed of superintendents who must be both committed as well as ultra-resilient. On-the-job stress has also increased considerably, resulting in more turnover, increased mobility, and shorter tenures within the role (Bjork & Keedy, 2003; Fenwick, 2000; Glatter, 1996; Henry, 2000; Natt, 2000). This, in turn, has resulted in a shortage of superintendents on the national level that is bordering on critical (Bjork & Keedy, 2003; Bjork & Kowalski, 2005; Hoyle, 2004; Natt, 2000). This shortage has, among other factors, created an increase in women and minority administrators (Krantz, 2000).

What, then, has become the role of the twenty-first-century superintendent, and what skills should the person in this position possess? What are the complexities of the changing roles within the superintendency, the quickly changing nature and responsibility of the top district leadership role, and changing contexts in which today's superintendents must work? What standards exist to help the superintendent become this "all things to all people" person? How were they developed, and what can they do to help superintendents not only survive but be successful in this increasingly changing and dynamic role? These are the questions we will answer in *Superintendent Leadership: Applying the Education Leadership Constituent Council Standards.*

WHAT SKILLS SHOULD A TWENTY-FIRST-CENTURY SUPERINTENDENT POSSESS?

Today's superintendents, above all, must become systems thinkers (Fullan, 2005; Hoyle, Bjork, Collier, & Glass, 2005). The superintendent must be able to understand the connection and alignment of all district dimensions while also understanding the relationship among the parts. In so doing, the superintendent must understand and build relationships among all the various district stakeholders. To be able to do this effectively, superintendents must understand and be able to guide the alignment of internal and external influences on the school system itself. Superintendents also need a deep understanding of change and the change process. The superintendent must have a certain set of knowledge, skills, and dispositions, or attitudes and, next, understand the influences they have on change in a school district. The school district includes the campuses themselves and the individuals impacted by decisions and actions of a school board that have been recommended by the superintendent.

To begin to do this, we can organize these traits into three categories as used by the National Council for the Accreditation of Teacher Education (NCATE). As shown in Figure 1.1, these are as follows:

Figure 1.1   Building Blocks for Superintendents

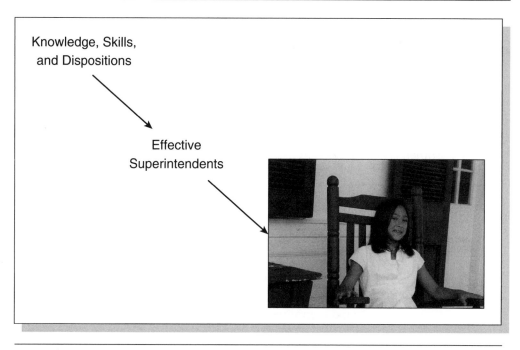

Source: Photo taken by Isabel Rendon-Peta

- ***Knowledge:*** What knowledge base should superintendents possess and utilize to be effective?
- ***Skills:*** What skills should superintendents have in dealing with people and organizations?
- ***Dispositions or Attitudes:*** What are the dispositions, or attitudes, that superintendents should display?

Indicators that superintendents are addressing the above knowledge, skills, and dispositions include, but certainly are not limited to, the following:

Knowledge

- Understanding the differentiation among the roles of teachers, principals, other administrators, the board of trustees, and the superintendent
- Understanding and applying curriculum and instructional theories that are developmentally appropriate for an increasingly diversified student population
- Being a strong business and academic leader
- Being fiscally prudent with both district and personal funds
- Being a "systems" thinker and problem solver

Skills

- Being both a consensus and team builder
- Having experience in prior positions of educational responsibility
- Needing and soliciting active community support
  - Being the voice of education in ever-widening circles
  - Soliciting an increase in support and active participation at all levels of district communications
  - Displaying professionalism with people who are constantly negative and/or creating problems
- Being responsible, because being a superintendent is an honorable responsibility
- Having the skills to work effectively with people from diverse communities
- Managing people well
- Exhibiting self-control in words and actions
  - Being nonviolent and managing anger even when justifiably provoked
- Being a good communicator and, thus, having the ability to motivate and teach others concepts they need to facilitate the district achieving its vision
- Supporting and encouraging change for district improvement and enhanced productivity and accountability
- Being able to handle work-related stress and pressure in a healthy and balanced manner

Dispositions

- Being committed to the value and truth of a well-rounded academic, cocurricular, and extracurricular education for all students
- Meriting the respect of others
  - Having a reputation such that those outside the immediate school community speak well of you
  - Having integrity and a character that is above reproach
  - Living wisely and with a clear conscience
  - Being faithful in all things, particularly to the cause of educating every student for an improved, free, and democratic society
- Displaying a healthy balance of confidence and humility in dealing with educational issues
- Having passion, wisdom, and the ability to facilitate the development, implementation, and evaluation of a district vision of learning

Superintendents who utilize such knowledge, skills, and dispositions will be rewarded with respect from others, increased student performance, confidence in their abilities, and success for their districts. Are these all of the necessary traits to be a successful superintendent today? Of course not. The above is not an all-inclusive list. It is a starting point at which a superintendent's experiences are combined with passion and dedication to create student success. Taken singly, these traits can be abstract concepts. Taken collectively, they can be integrated into a workable model for superintendent leadership, as will be presented in the following chapters. This was the goal of the Educational Leadership Constituent Council (ELCC) as it brought together varying professional groups and organizations to synthesize their different standards into a practical, workable set upon which all superintendents, in both public and private schools, could generate success.

Pressing questions for us are these:

- Exactly what are the ELCC standards?
- How were they developed?
- How can you and others utilize them to create and connect to realistic practice that will maximize student and district performance?

HISTORY AND DEVELOPMENT OF THE EDUCATIONAL LEADERSHIP CONSTITUENT COUNCIL STANDARDS

For years, multiple sets of standards have existed for both superintendent and principal development. Although some of the standards were similar, there was no one concise set upon which the major professional administrator organizations and educational leadership professorial groups could agree. In 1994, the National Policy Board for Educational Administration (NPBEA), already well known for its own 21 domains, created the Interstate School Leaders Licensure Consortium (ISLLC) to bring the various stakeholders together. The mission was to create one set of collaboratively developed and agreed-upon standards. Funding for the project was subsequently obtained from the Pew Charitable Trusts and the Danforth Foundation. From 1994 to 1996, the ISLLC Consortium worked to create and seek input on this initial set of standards, which subsequently became known as the ISLLC Standards. In 1996, the National Policy Board adopted these standards, which were then published by the Council of Chief State School Officers (CCSSO), the group that consists of and represents the top educational agency representatives in each state.

In the meantime, the independent Educational Leadership Constituent Council (ELCC) was developed primarily by the American Association of School Administrators (AASA), the American Association for Supervision and Curriculum Development (ASCD), the National Association of

Secondary School Principals (NASSP), and the National Association of Elementary School Principals (NAESP) (Wilmore, 2002). This group utilized the ISLLC Standards to develop the Standards for Advanced Programs in Educational Leadership (www.ncate.org). The ELCC set added the seventh standard, which addresses the preparation of future superintendents and principals (www.npbea.org/ELCC/ELCCStandards%20_5–02.pdf). The most striking, and some say most important, feature of the seventh standard is its focus on a year-long internship collaboratively developed among the university, the district field setting, and the student. While both the NPBEA and the National Council for Accreditation of Teacher Education (NCATE) had their own, sometimes differing, opinions, the full set of ELCC standards was adopted by the NCATE in 2001. Since that time, school administrator preparation programs seeking to obtain NCATE accreditation have gone through an intense assessment process based on these ELCC standards.

In education, rarely does anything stay the same. During 2003–2005, CCSSO formed another subgroup, the Interstate Consortium on School Leadership (ICSL), which was charged with more adequately defining "highly qualified administrators" in accordance with the No Child Left Behind Act (NCLB). This charge came as a response from various state policy makers who were requesting assistance in clarifying this somewhat elusive issue (Sanders & Simpson, 2006). Exactly what constitutes a highly qualified administrator? One of the ways determined to do this was to research and update the ISLLC and ELCC standards, which by then were serving their purpose as national models for administrator preparation (ELCC) and performance-based assessment of practicing administrators (ISLLC). ICSL took on this in-depth task in conjunction with the National Policy Board for Educational Administration. In 2006, the NPBEA Steering Committee developed and approved the model by which the updating of the ISLLC and ELCC standards would take place. Input was sought from various segments, including the original four administrator professional organizations plus the University Council for Educational Administration (UCEA), the National Council for Professors of Educational Administration (NCPEA), and multiple practitioners in the field. This model continues in use as the standards refinement process progresses.

WHAT ARE THE ELCC STANDARDS?

As shown in Figure 1.2, there are seven ELCC standards. The seventh standard is primarily intended for universities and alternative preparation programs to utilize as a guide in creating a collaborative and successful year-long internship for administrators preparing to become, in this case, superintendents. The focus of each standard is to maximize student learning.

Figure 1.2   The Educational Leadership Constituent Council Standards Focus on Student Success

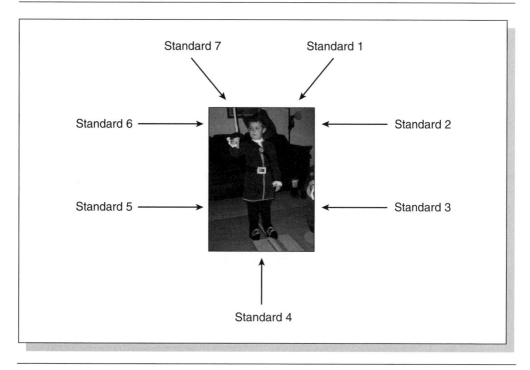

Source: Photo taken by Emily Rollen

The full set of standards is as follows:

Standard 1. A school district leader who has the knowledge and ability to promote the success of all students by facilitating the development, articulation, implementation, and stewardship of a school or district vision of learning that is supported by the school community

Standard 2. A school district leader who has the knowledge and ability to promote the success of all students by promoting a positive school culture, providing an effective instructional program, applying best practices to student learning, and designing comprehensive professional growth plans for staff

Standard 3. A school district leader who has the knowledge and ability to promote the success of all students by managing the organization, operations, and resources in a way that promotes a safe, efficient, and effective learning environment

Standard 4. A school district leader who has the knowledge and ability to promote the success of all students by collaborating with families and other community members, responding to diverse community interests and needs, and mobilizing community resources

Standard 5. A school district leader who has the knowledge and ability to promote the success of all students by acting with integrity and fairness and in an ethical manner

Standard 6. A school district leader who has the knowledge and ability to promote the success of all students by understanding, responding to, and influencing the larger political, social, economic, legal, and cultural context

Standard 7. The internship provides significant opportunities for candidates to synthesize and apply the knowledge and practice and develop the skills identified in Standards 1–6 through substantial, sustained, standards-based work in real settings, planned and guided cooperatively by the institution and school district personnel for graduate credit.

CREATING THE CONNECTION BETWEEN THE ELCC STANDARDS AND REALISTIC PRACTICE

By utilizing the ELCC-ISLLC standards as a model upon which to focus decision making and subsequent action, superintendents can rely upon the research that has been developed by the multiple "constituents" involved in development of the standards. This book seeks to connect the collaboratively developed concepts within the standards to practical application in real schools and districts today. The standards provide a research base that superintendents and other district-level leaders can use to improve relationships within the district and with the school board and to create a learning community, resulting in improved student performance and organizational leadership. No longer will "All students can learn" be something people say but may not totally believe. All students can learn if provided the right motivation, support, and developmentally appropriate curriculum and instructional strategies that meet their needs and are relevant to their lives. Obviously, this is easier said than done. It is the quest we all share. Will this ever be easy? Probably not. Few things worth achieving are ever easy. Yet our goal is that with hard work, commitment to the cause, creativity, persistence, and lots of resiliency, superintendents can lead districts to improve learning for all students. In the end, isn't that what education is all about?

THE ROLE OF THE SUPERINTENDENT IN A CHANGING DEMOCRATIC SOCIETY

Without a doubt, the world today is changing (Berman, 2005). Sometimes, it seems this is happening faster than we can keep up with.

Thus, it is easy to become bogged down, even overwhelmed, with the pressure pushing in on us in an increasingly demanding manner. Data shows that superintendents leave their current positions earlier than they might have desired and that some leave the profession altogether (Czaja & Harman, 1997). Combined, these trends create a nation where there are not enough solid superintendents to go around (Bjork & Keedy, 2003; Bjork & Kowalski, 2005; Bowler, 2000; Glatter, 1996; Natt, 2000; Tingly, 1996). The ELCC standards are not intended to be rules that will magically solve all problems. They are intended to be guidelines upon which superintendents and other district leaders can "hang their hats"—to hold onto tightly as a guidance model in this ever-changing world.

Is it easy to be the CEO of a school district? Definitely not. But are the results worth it if the job is done correctly? Absolutely! That is what the ELCC standards are for. They are guideposts, or benchmarks, to help us along our way as we seek to improve our ever-changing society by utilizing a strong research base.

Will this be easy? No.

Is it achievable? Yes, without a doubt. Read on, and let's see how to do it.

It's All About the Vision

"Go confidently in the direction of your dreams. Live the life you've imagined."

—Henry David Thoreau

> **Standard 1:** A school district leader who has the knowledge and ability to promote the success of all students by facilitating the development, articulation, implementation, and stewardship of a school or district vision of learning that is supported by the school community

INTRODUCTION

On Monday, January 8, 2007, 13-year-old Ben Ownby got off the school bus to walk the remaining short distance to his Missouri home. But young Ben did not make it home that day—or for nearly a week thereafter. Ben was kidnapped. Thanks in large part to his neighbor and fellow bus rider, Mitchell Hults, 15, Ben's family, community, and police got an excellent description of a white truck that was seen driving fast at the approximate time of the kidnapping. Four days later, Ben was found safe and alive in suburban St. Louis, Missouri.

What police did not expect when they found Ben was Shawn Hornbeck being there also. Shawn had been abducted over four years previously when he was 11 years old. Media commentators called the joint rescue a "twofer," as two boys were found when authorities thought they were closing in on only one.

While the experiences of the two boys are equally heartrending, the stories from both families are the true definition of love, joy, and sheer ecstatic relief. The following day, both sets of parents gave press conferences jointly with law enforcement officials. Craig Akers, Shawn's stepfather, was particularly eloquent as he fought back tears while retelling their long, relentless four-year journey to search for Shawn. Yet, Akers said, the family never gave up. They were firm in their commitment to keep searching till Shawn was found. They established the Shawn Hornbeck Foundation to continue looking for him and for other exploited children. Even though logic would suggest that the family would never see Shawn again, since he had been gone such an extraordinarily long time, still they refused to give up hope. Shawn's family had a passionate vision of having their son back. Anyone viewing the January 13, 2007, press conference could see the miraculous results of an unrelenting vision even when faced with what had seemed like an impossible situation.

For educators, and especially for superintendents, it is imperative that we have that same tunnel-vision relentlessness and passion toward never giving up on providing a solid education for every student. Often, private schools can be selective about who they admit. Public schools cannot. Public schools must enroll Attila the Hun if he shows up. If Attila does not speak the dominant language, has learning problems, dyes his hair purple, sports multiple body piercings and tattoos, and doesn't seem to care if he is there or not, public schools must still enroll him. It is easy to get tired and discouraged when thinking about how Attila will fare under No Child Left Behind (NCLB) regulations. Yet today's superintendents lead the charge of creating school district cultures and environments that are conducive to every student's maximizing learning productivity. Today's superintendents often do this with less than adequate funding, not enough highly qualified teachers, and, sometimes, without the total support of the taxpayers. Yet we forge on, never giving up. We do this because *we have the vision!*

As shown in Figure 2.1, standards-based superintendents

- develop a district vision;
- articulate the district vision;

Figure 2.1 Standards-Based Superintendents Are Visionaries

- Develop a district vision.
- Articulate the district vision.
- Implement the district vision.
- Are good stewards of the district vision.

Source: Photo taken by Elizabeth Hall

- implement the district vision; and
- act as good stewards of the district vision.

PHILOSOPHICAL FRAMEWORK

Developing a District Vision

One of the first and most important roles of a superintendent is to establish, implement, and continually assess and update a district vision of learning that is based on solid research (Hoyle, 2006; Hoyle et al., 2005). There is no way to overemphasize how important the district vision is. It is the focus, the benchmark, by which all district decision making should be measured. Without a solid vision of where the district wants to be, the superintendent can end up moving from day to day in a management role instead of a true leadership role. As shown in Figure 2.2, the purpose of the district vision is to move the district from today's reality to tomorrow's ideal.

That, of course, is not to undermine the importance of solid district management, which will be addressed largely in Standard 3. However, with a good balance of both management and leadership, the district will maximize its decision-making effectiveness and resources while maximizing its productivity.

Figure 2.2   District Improvement Process: Moving From Reality to the District Vision

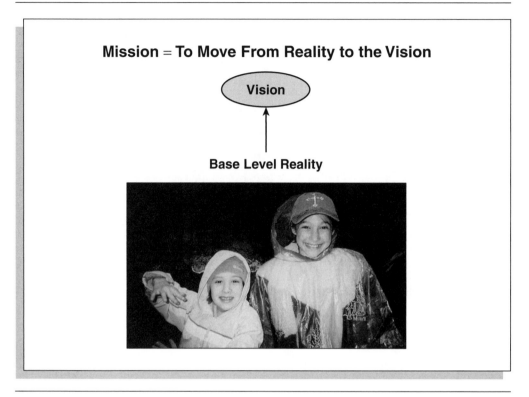

Source: Photo taken by Isabel Rendon-Peta

Figure 2.3   Vision and Goal-Setting Alignment: All Goals Should Support the District Vision

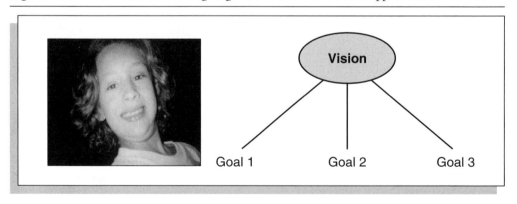

Source: Photo taken by Isabel Rendon-Peta

Figure 2.3 illustrates that everything the district seeks to accomplish must be aligned to this vision. Thus, the vision must be created and agreed upon as soon as possible. Therefore, the superintendent must have the necessary skills to create a systematic vision that gives individual scenarios meaning and connects them to what might become a system/district vision.

The process of creating a vision can differ greatly, depending on how the superintendent understands and works within the district context as it exists and may evolve. Creating an effective vision must be based on long-range strategic planning, where multiple constituencies and stakeholders are involved and invested in its development, implementation, and evaluation. A maximally enhanced district vision results from the planning process by which the vision was developed. Central to all of this is the superintendent's relationship and shared governance with the board of education. It is important that this not be "the superintendent's vision" but one that has been put together with the input of as many constituencies and stakeholders of the district as possible. People will support what they help create. They may not be nearly as inclined to support a vision in which they feel absolutely no ownership. Everyone will have distinct ideas, and each of them will be important.

Synthesizing divergent viewpoints into a vision upon which everyone can agree takes time, cooperation, and guidance in consensus building. It is not possible to throw together a meaningful vision with a small group of people one afternoon after school when everyone is tired. Developing the vision takes time, effort, hard work, and positive give-and-take. Critical to success is finding the issues on which the group can agree rather than disagree. Figure 2.4 shows how varying perspectives can intersect to identify the basic issues and the common ground upon which they agree.

Figure 2.4   Identifying and Respecting the Common Ground

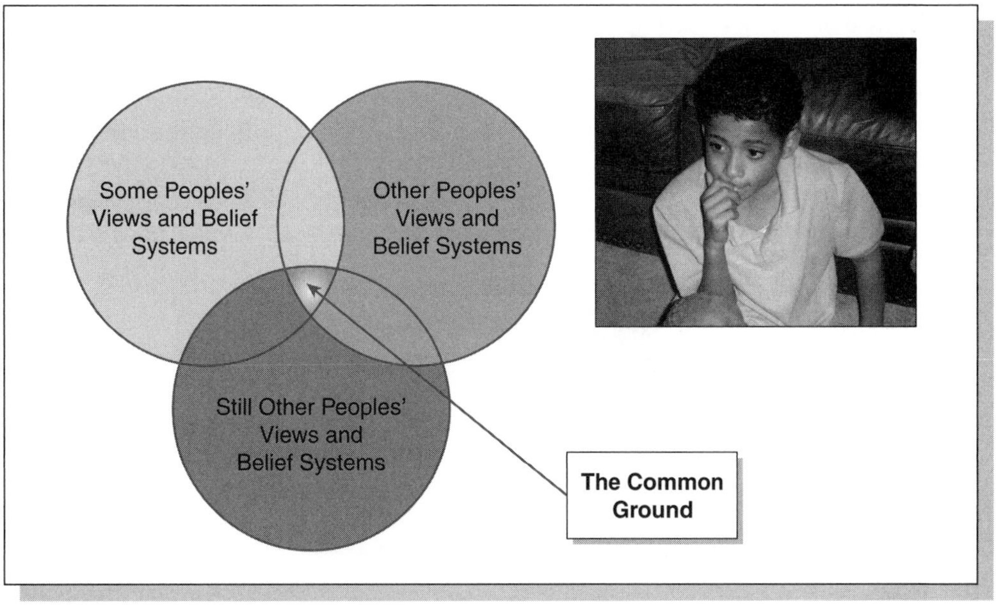

Source: Quincey & Kimberley Miller

Identifying common ground is the starting point for developing and identifying a district vision that focuses on creating learning and success for each district student. Everything else the district does should be aligned with helping it achieve this vision of productivity. As shown in Figure 2.5, each district goal, objective, strategies for attainment, and assessment thereof must be aligned with the district vision.

After a common base of perspectives is identified, the superintendent and board make decisions regarding the vision based on their knowledge of district data, facts, and theories in the same manner that principals study student data for their campuses. However, decisions are based on what is best for the entire district rather than for an individual campus. This broader scope is harder both to discern and deal with. Systems thinking is an important and necessary element. Superintendents must be cautious to make sure all campuses and units are empowered and facilitated to meet their own goals, which should be mutually aligned with the district vision and goals.

Figure 2.5 Align District Activities With Specific Goals That Lead to the Vision

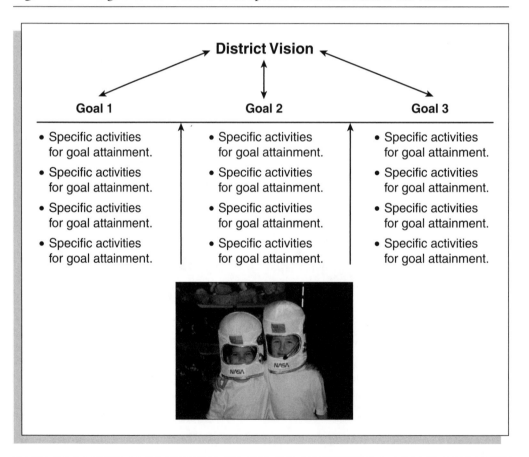

Source: Michael & Karen Fawcett

When studying district data, superintendents and boards utilize research-based strategies in working with vision development to ensure that the diversity of district learners and learning styles is well represented and addressed. Different students come from different cultures and environments. Even students from within the same subgroups have diverse issues to deal with. Targeting curricular and instructional designs in a manner to help each student succeed can seem like an insurmountable task. Yet the district vision must incorporate this array of diversity in its inception, implementation, evaluation, and refinement.

Another major issue that superintendents and boards must consider while developing the vision is how to fund it. So many districts suffer from a lack of money to be do everything needed for students. School districts are usually tied to state financial formulas in regard to how money is distributed, making fulfilling a vision challenging. Going even further, district hands are also often tied by the threat of "roll-back" elections if they raise local taxes above a certain amount. All of this complicates developing the budget necessary to meet the district vision and goals. Because of this, superintendents must continually watch for various forms of external funding, including federal assistance and grants, and ways to maximize and prioritize existing monies.

The same is also true for all district resources, not just funding. Maximizing the benefit of educator talents—for example, reducing time-consuming tasks that are not absolutely necessary, such as repetitive paperwork and meetings—is important. For educators to do their jobs effectively, they must have freedom, with guidance, to do what they need to do to get the job done. For this reason, superintendents constantly search for new ways to mobilize additional resources to support the district vision as well as to reduce redundancy, free up educator time, and maximize efficiency.

Articulating the District Vision

Once the district vision has been developed, the next step is to articulate it effectively both inside the district and outside in the greater school community. It doesn't do a lot of good to have a marvelous, research-based vision if people do not know about it, how it was developed, why it is important, what their role in it needs to be, and what is in it both for them and for the district at large. Frequently, much time and effort is put into developing the vision, yet it never gets implemented as it should because it was never clearly and effectively communicated to everyone who needs to know, understand, support, and implement it. Therefore, articulating the vision effectively is every bit as important as developing and putting it into place.

The superintendent and leadership team must have the necessary guidance and communication skills to ensure that all stakeholders know and understand the importance of the vision and their role in it. Each piece of the vision, each goal as well as proposed implementation strategies and assessments, must be clearly communicated in ways that people understand. The school community must know the strategic planning and research that went into its development, including student data, quantitative and qualitative assessments, and various forms of student and family demographic data; and a school community needs assessment and analysis of the results. All of this is done to make the best decisions possible to improve student learning.

Although some superintendents are more articulate and/or charismatic than others, each must find a way of ensuring that the vision is conveyed so that it can be understood by multiple stakeholders, including the school board, staff, parents, students, and community members. Communication can be done both personally and through others. It can be implemented through the use of symbols, ceremonies, stories, and other activities. The important thing is not how the vision is communicated but that it is communicated so that everyone can understand it.

Implementing the District Vision

Once the vision is developed and appropriately communicated, it is ready for implementation. It is important to remember not to rush the process. Do not start the great things that have been planned until everyone knows what is going on and why. If you try to save time on this step, you will lose it later in the effort of recommunicating what was not appropriately communicated in the first place. In simple language, make sure everyone knows what is going on. Save yourself the grief and the talking behind your back when people say, "What on earth is going on around here?" Take care of communication and role responsibilities up front. Then you can move on to the actual implementation of the vision.

You will know the vision is being implemented in the correct ways throughout the district when the research-based processes previously determined are put into place both inside and outside the schools. Superintendents are not responsible for doing each tiny step themselves. However, they are responsible for being the facilitators of ensuring that each step gets done efficiently and effectively. They are also responsible for having programs in place that will motivate others, including the staff, students, and families, in working together to achieve the district vision.

Being a Good Steward of the District Vision

For many people, the words *steward* or *stewardship* have a religious connotation, wherein people seek to be good "stewards" of church money and resources and exercise good "stewardship" through their tithes and offerings. Obviously, there are many ways to interpret being a good steward, but a useful correlation can be made between the words in a religious context and in the context of an educational system. Superintendents must be good stewards of the district money and resources. But they must also be good stewards of the district's vision.

If the right groundwork is done in the development, articulation, and implementation of the district vision, putting it into place should get off to a good start. However, educators, families, community members, and, yes, even superintendents themselves are only human. Sooner or later, we can all start to wear down. We get tired. We can have a tendency simply to go through the motions because we have so many pressures all around us. This does not mean we are no longer committed to the vision. It means we are human and we are tired. Eventually, everyone needs some time to sit back, reflect, think about what is taking place, assess it, determine how things could be done better, and refocus personally and professionally before moving on. There is nothing wrong with taking this time. Reflective assessment is one way of being a good steward of the vision. It is important to remember that needing this downtime is a normal human process. It is also important to utilize what you learn from it not just to pick yourself up when you are down, tired, or worn out but also to be there, as a good steward, for other district educators and community members when they are going through the same thing.

An important component of this reflective process is research and evaluation. Each piece of the vision must be under constant assessment, continuously asking, "How can we do this better?" Nothing should be exempt from this process. Each and every thing being done in the district should be aligned with the district vision. As such, it needs to be monitored, assessed, and modified based on results.

Promoting Community Involvement in the District Vision

It is one thing to have a district vision, even when many people have been involved in its research and development. It is something else entirely to get as many facets of the community as possible to support it in both word and deed. Whether in regard to supporting school district planning or that of cities, counties, states, or various issues on the national level, it seems as though in today's society, more and more citizens are just against virtually anything that comes up. They may be against an idea because they are afraid it will raise their taxes, albeit ever so slightly. They may be against it for philosophical, social, cultural, or faith-based reasons. Or they just may be against anything whatsoever it may be for no good reason other than enjoying their minute in the limelight for being against something.

If the district wants to adopt the lowest bid for school milk prices, they are against it. They claim that students should bring their milk from home. If the district needs to add to or replace the existing bus fleet, they are against it. "Parents should bring their own children to school," they say.

Obviously, those citizens have issues far beyond the insights of this book. A former school board trustee and friend of mine, Dean Woodruff, calls them "CAVE People." His version of CAVE stands for:

C = Citizens
A = Against
V = Virtually
E = Everything

If you are new to the field, you may think these people do not exist. If you have been in the field very long, you know that not only do they exist, they seem to be multiplying faster than the speed of light.

In an ideal world, if a vision of learning has been collaboratively developed, articulated, and implemented, superintendents would have already worked with multiple constituencies within the community to communicate exactly what has been decided, why the decision(s) were made, what resources will be needed, how it will be evaluated, and how the community at large can be of help. Those are the days we live for! Often, it is not quite that easy. Superintendents, and all educators, must continue to be good stewards of the vision and articulate the vision effectively even when times are tough. We celebrate the good times, and we hang tough together during the not-so-good times. But we never, ever give up. The vision of the district is the core of everything we seek to accomplish. Therefore, we invite, solicit, and do everything we can creatively and ethically to encourage the larger school community to support and be actively engaged in helping us help others. To this end, we never despair. We may get tired, frustrated, and depressed. But we never give up. We stay on-message, communicating the importance of a free and appropriate education for every child in every district and our responsibility as communities in a free and democratic society to provide every student exactly that.

PROBLEM-BASED LEARNING

Developing and Articulating a District Vision: Where Are We Going to Put So Many New Students?

The Rapides Parish School District is faced with a fast growth rate, in large part due to an influx of immigrants from Mexico and elsewhere in Latin America. Several schools that were already full to capacity have had to bring in portable buildings. Some campuses that already have portable buildings do not have room to bring in more. At the same time, the district has several elementary campuses with some extra available classroom space. The district is not wealthy and has not yet participated in any kind of strategic planning to address the rapidly growing and increasingly diverse student population.

Now, with some campuses overflowing, Superintendent Daniel Massimo is faced with the unhappy prospect of talking to his school board about what to do with the schools that are exceeding capacity and the ones that are not quite full as well as the district not having enough money to meet student facility needs within the current framework.

Before meeting with the school board, Daniel reviewed the academic performance of the district over the past several years. He noted a downward trend in standardized test scores, particularly among the immigrant students. Daniel is concerned that the needs of all students are not being appropriately met. He is resolved to work closely with the school board to develop and articulate a new vision of learning, which will focus on the needs of the district's changing population as well as addressing the pressing need for better facilities management and long-term strategic planning. He knows facilities changes are necessary but also realizes that change is not always popular. He is aware that the idea of changing attendance zones may upset families who are comfortable at certain schools. However, he also knows that the idea of busing students or building new campuses will meet with disapproval. Frankly, Daniel isn't quite sure how to proceed and is dreading telling his board that very thing.

Reflective Practice: Pause and Think

Through the use of reflection and higher-order thinking skills:

1. Describe a strategic planning process by which Daniel and the school board can take a holistic, systematic look at the district's growth issues, the academic performance of all students, and the development and articulation of a new district vision.

2. What types of research data should Daniel and the school board analyze before making any decisions? Why?

3. What groups of people should the superintendent and school board be sure to include in the planning process? Why?

4. Brainstorm options the superintendent and board should consider in addressing this problem for both the short and long term. Discuss the pros and cons of each.

5. If the decision is made to redraw attendance zones to maximize the capacity of existing facilities, what steps should be taken to ensure balance and diversity of administrators, faculty, staff, and students on each campus?

6. How can the superintendent ensure that the greater district community is knowledgeable about the issues and solicited to play a part in creating a vision of learning for the changing and expanding district demographics?

Implementing and Being a Good Steward of the District Vision: Let's Try This One More Time

Like the Rapides Parish School District, the Wimberley Falls Independent School District is also experiencing growth. Theirs, however, is not the rapid growth such as Rapides is experiencing. The Wimberley Falls growth is slower and more sustained. Superintendent Sharron Martin has faithfully been watching this growth for several years and knows the time is coming when the district will need to expand existing facilities. In an attempt to be proactive, she is keeping her school board current on this growth and its implications for the district as times goes by. They all agree that sooner or later, a time will come when some difficult decisions regarding adding on to existing campuses, building new ones, and/or the possibility of closing at least two very old buildings will have to be addressed.

The board and Sharron decide to hire a growth consultant who was recommended to them through their state affiliate of the American Association of School Administrators. The consultant spent several months off and on in the district, visiting existing schools, visiting potential new campus sites within the district, visiting with various educators and citizens, and studying demographic patterns and growth trends. Based on the consultant's recommendation, the board voted to call for a bond election, whereby citizens could vote for or against two "facilities packages," combinations of renovations and additions to existing facilities and the construction of three new ones. The third option that citizens could vote for was "against any changes." In other words, people who voted for this option did not want to do anything at all, regardless of the need. They were just "against."

The third option of citizens being against everything won. Sharron and the school board were horrified at this outcome. They could not believe that after all their hard work, as well as the work of an outside consultant, the citizens of their district would vote against any renovations, additions, or new construction at all.

As they followed up on the election results, they learned several things that they wished they had learned before the election. First, they learned that most of the district felt totally disenfranchised from the process. Although facts were given to them, they were never involved in the planning process. Because Wimberley Falls's growth rate was slow and steady, they simply did not see the large visible differences in sheer numbers that the citizens of Rapides Parish could see. They also learned that there was a small, but distinct, segment of the community that was absolutely and totally opposed to any building project that would close the two oldest campuses. They believed those campuses were better built than many of the newer ones and that they had withstood the test of time better than any new buildings ever could. Besides, they were sentimentally attached to the older buildings because, after all, they had been there *forever*, even way back when Grandpappy was walking to school in the snow.

Equipped with all this new information, the Board decided to call a second election with a different combination of packages from which voters could chose. This time, though, they brought in citizens from all segments of the community, including those who were opposed to closing the older campuses, and showed them the facts, including student growth rates and other valuable information. This time, they empowered the community group to develop better solutions and packages than were originally presented. Consequently, the board and superintendent listened rather than coming up with the plans themselves. After long months of conflict resolution, the citizens' committee came up with two sets of plans that they could enthusiastically support. Armed with this strong community support from diverse stakeholders, the school board again called for a bond election with the packages on the ballot that the citizens committee recommended. To their great relief, the second bond election passed.

Reflective Practice: Pause and Think

1. Identify mistakes the superintendent and school board made in the planning, articulation, and implementation of the first bond election.

2. What implementation steps were taken with the second election to improve the outcome?

3. Why were these steps necessary to fulfill the vision of appropriate district facilities for all students?

4. How did the superintendent act as a steward of the vision between the two elections?

5. What other steps could the superintendent have taken prior to the calling of the first bond election to involve the community more and better articulate the need for future planning?

6. Develop a strategic plan that includes solutions to potential problems that could arise in your own district if a bond election became necessary.

Promoting Community Involvement
in the District Vision: But . . . We Used
to Win All the Time! What's Going On?

The Litchfield Beach School District was used to winning football games. In fact, they were used to winning basketball games, baseball games, track meets, and anything else that came along. As girls sports gained popularity, the fine citizens of Litchfield Beach jumped right in and supported their volleyball team and cheered their girls all the way to the state softball tournament. In case you haven't figured it out, Litchfield Beach likes to win. The only thing they like better than winning is winning big.

For the last several years, the football team has not been doing so well. It all started two years ago with that new coach, Bryant Grey. Bryant came in with a lot of big talk about winning the state football championship right away. He even went so far as to say he was going to start answering the telephone, "Win State!" regardless of who was calling. The fine folks of Litchfield Beach liked his attitude and thought this young man was going to fit into the culture of Litchfield Beach just fine.

Unfortunately, things didn't work out quite so well. During the first game, the team got clobbered. It was a humbling experience for the team and citizens because they didn't like to lose, much less get clobbered. Eye brows went up all over town. Practices were heated the next week because Coach Grey knew getting clobbered again was not going to work in Litchfield Beach.

Well, they got clobbered again. The following week, they got clobbered again. Let's just say it was a very difficult season. Superintendent Henry Crabtree could hardly go out in public for people blasting him about that idiot football coach he hired. Superintendent Crabtree took those as fighting words because, after all, he was a former football coach himself. Still, he stood by his man and assured everyone that next year would be better. "It just takes a while to instill your program and get the team going your way," he explained to the citizens. The community wasn't real sure they believed him, but they were willing to give Coach Gray another chance since they were, after all, such fine folks.

The second year was only slightly better than the first. The team did manage to squeak out a few victories, but the rest of the season was hard to take. By now, the town was pumped up enough to want to run Coach Grey, and possibly Superintendent Crabtree also, out of town on a rail. This losing business was simply not going to work in Litchfield Beach!

Sometimes it is good to have the community totally engaged in what is going on within the school district. Having two years of a losing football team certainly had Litchfield Beach engaged, but not in a positive direction. Henry and the school board were being blasted everywhere to get rid of that crazy coach and bring back ol' Coach Neely who retired about five years ago. "At least with Coach Neely, our team used to win! We want to win again! What part of 'expecting to win' do you not understand?" they repeatedly asked—and sometimes yelled—at Henry and the school board.

Reflective Practice: Pause and Think

1. What part, if any, should athletics and other co- and extracurricular activities play in the vision of the district and school community?

2. Should the superintendent pay attention to the screaming masses who want Coach Grey fired? If so, in what way(s)?

3. Upon occasion, a district's citizens can get unduly worked up over an issue that is not as big a deal as they feel that it is. In those instances, how should a superintendent handle the situation?

4. What other ways of rechanneling the district's energies can a proactive superintendent utilize to defuse a potentially explosive situation?

5. Develop and describe a conflict resolution methodology whereby citizens enraged about any issue can be brought into being part of the solution to a problem rather than being its focus.

6. What would you do if you were superintendent of Litchfield Beach? How would you handle this volatile situation?

ASSESSMENT MODEL

Standard 1: A school district leader who has the knowledge and ability to promote the success of all students by facilitating the development, articulation, implementation, and stewardship of a school or district vision of learning supported by the school community

In Table 2.1, you will find a planning rubric for assessing your progress toward this standard. Vertical and horizontal mentoring are important elements in maximizing your success. For additional reading on administrator induction and mentoring, see *Principal Induction: A Standards-Based Model for Administrator Development* (Wilmore, 2004).

Table 2.1 Planning Rubric for Standard 1

Element	Goals to Meet Standard for Improved School District Leadership	Specific Activities Designed to Achieve Standard	People and Resources Necessary to Operationalize This Strategy	Date by Which Activity Will Be Completed	Evidence of Standard Attainment
1.1 Develop a Vision	a. Develop and demonstrate the skills needed to work with a board of education to facilitate the development of a vision of learning for a school district that promotes the success of all students.				
	b. Develop the vision based on relevant knowledge and theories applicable to school-level leaders as applied to a school district context.				
	c. Utilize data-based research strategies to create a vision that takes into account the diversity of learners in a district.				
	d. Demonstrate knowledge of ways to use a district's vision to mobilize additional resources to support the vision.				
1.2 Articulate a Vision	a. Demonstrate the ability to articulate the components of the vision for a district and the leadership processes necessary to implement and support the vision.				
	b. Demonstrate the ability to use data-based research strategies and strategic planning processes that focus on student learning to develop a vision, drawing on relevant information sources such as student assessment results, student and family demographic data, and an analysis of community needs.				

	c. Demonstrate the ability to communicate the vision to school boards, staff, parents, students, and community members through the use of symbols, ceremonies, stories, and other activities.				
1.3 Implement a Vision	a. Demonstrate the ability to plan programs to motivate staff, students, and families to achieve a school district's vision.				
	b. Design research-based processes to implement effectively a district vision throughout an entire school district and community.				
1.4 Steward a Vision	a. Demonstrate the ability to align and, as necessary, redesign administrative policies and practices required for full implementation of a district vision.				
	b. Understand the theory and research related to organizational and educational leadership and engage in the collection, organization, and analysis of a variety of information, including student performance data, required to assess progress toward a district's vision, mission, and goals.				
1.5 Promote Community Involvement in the Vision	a. Demonstrate the ability to bring together and communicate effectively with stakeholders within the district and the larger community concerning implementation and realization of the vision.				

Ways for You to Do It:

A superintendent leader can enhance systematic school improvement by using the following strategies:

- Basing all decisions on what is best for the students rather than what is convenient or cheaper for the district
- Realizing that each campus and student is different and meeting the needs of each one versus utilizing a "one size fits all" standardization mentality, particularly when comparing campuses
- Actively soliciting and valuing teacher and community input on as many issues as reasonably possible, including setting reasonable goals
- Spending more time visiting campuses and classrooms as well as being visibly and actively engaged in the school community
- Staying current on state and federal financial issues to maximize district external funding
- Supporting improved campus discipline management and enhanced teacher and administrator training
- Empowering all district educators to improve their knowledge, skills, and dispositions and providing adequate funding for them to do so
- When realistic efforts made to improve teacher, staff, or administrator performance prove unsuccessful, solving the problem by removing the underperforming employee from the position
- Proactively seeking to understand and meet the needs of students from diverse backgrounds as well as those who are learning English, in special education, and, particularly, those who "fall between the cracks" and do not qualify for special education

CONCLUSIONS

There is simply no way to overemphasize the importance of a coherently and collaboratively developed vision for the school district that is shared and supported by all stakeholders. A strong case could be made that developing such a vision in this way is the first and foremost task of the superintendent. The vision is not something that is developed once to say you did it, then neatly printed into various documents only to be reviewed periodically. It is the guiding focus by which all district decisions should be made. It should be updated and enhanced continuously based upon the best available data and progress toward district goals and attainment. The vision is the instrument by which we measure student performance.

It should be collaboratively developed with the district board of trustees with significant input from as many school community segments as possible, because people support what they help create. A targeted effort should be made to include voices from all subgroups and populations within the district. Once developed, the vision should be clearly and consistently articulated throughout the school community such that everyone knows what it is, how it was developed, why it is important, what their role in it is, and how it will be assessed.

The needs of all students must be addressed at all times. Instruction should be engaging and relevant to learners who will be motivated to learn rather than having a top-down mentality of "This is what you need to know." Students want and deserve to know why they need to learn anything as well as how it can help them be successful in their daily lives now and for the future.

When times are tough, particularly in districts that are experiencing fast growth or other forms of rapid change, the superintendent's responsibility is to be the steward of the vision, to help people stay on task, and always to be the voice for the importance of the district vision as it applies to the value of education for all students in a free and democratic society. The stewardship of the vision pertains to fiscal and personnel management also, for we would be nothing without our teachers, staff, other administrators, and the necessary means to move us along our continuous journey toward vision attainment.

The Ultimate Application

The following questions are designed to assist you in applying higher-level thinking skills through application. Either alone or in a group setting, respond to each question based upon your own knowledge, experience, and further research.

1. Describe a process you would utilize for creating a vision statement with ownership from all stakeholders in the district learning community.

2. Prepare a hypothetical vision statement for your current school district.

3. Once a district vision is developed, in what ways could you facilitate its articulation and communication inside and outside the district?

4. Why is it important for district goals to be developed collaboratively instead of by the superintendent alone?

5. Compare and contrast districts with, and without, an identified and targeted vision. What differences would you likely see?

6. What exactly is the difference between a district vision and district goals?

7. Describe and discuss the importance of alignment of the district vision and goals with curriculum, instruction, assessment, resources, budgets, and staff professional development.

8. Create a case study that demonstrates the alignment process.

3

Advocating, Nurturing, and Sustaining Enhanced Student Learning and Staff Professional Growth

"If you do it right, you can teach the whole world to dance."

—Pat Conroy

Standard 2: A school district leader who has the knowledge and ability to promote the success of all students by promoting a positive school culture, providing an effective instructional program, applying best practices to student learning, and designing comprehensive professional growth plans for staff

INTRODUCTION

Many years back, more years than I care to remember, our family was preparing to move across the state. In preparation for this move, we decided to have a garage sale and get rid of as many things as possible that we no longer needed. Our three children were still in elementary school, so we had plenty of their clothes and toys amid the other articles we were hoping to sell.

On the day of the garage sale, my father-in-law came over to help. We had a fun day meeting new people, ordering hamburgers for lunch, and, yes, selling a *lot* of stuff. As the day drew to a close, my father-in-law commented about what a good day we'd had. He laughingly said he had never seen anyone sell used children's socks before and the buyers feeling so good about it!

Isn't that what we are doing in leading and "selling" our nation's schools? Aren't we marketing to the public and our students the value of a quality education for individuals as well as for our nation and society as a whole? Some do better than others at communicating this. We all want citizens not just to understand and "buy" the merits of a good education but also to feel good about it. We do this by creating an environment where teachers can teach and students can learn. As shown in Figure 3.1, we will address four specific core concepts not only to help us achieve these goals but to help America feel good about them.

Figure 3.1 Standards-Based Superintendents Provide Leadership

- Promote a positive school culture.

- Provide an effective instructional program.

- Apply best practices for student learning.

- Design comprehensive professional growth plans.

Source: Courtesy of Lee, Alison, & Elizabeth Hefley

PHILOSOPHICAL FRAMEWORK

Promoting a Positive District Culture

Having a district and campus culture and climate that are conducive to teachers being able to teach effectively and where students are actively engaged in learning is critical to the success of the district as a whole. While some may think of the district culture and climate as "soft" elements, you won't think they are soft if you are entrenched in controversy and working in an adversarial atmosphere with other educators or the school community. That is when you need culture and climate the most. While important, they are often left to chance. As positive and proactive superintendents, we cannot afford to leave anything to chance. We must look at every facet of the learning community to determine where our needs are, then research directly what is needed and how to provide it to optimize learning.

So what exactly are district, or organizational, culture and climate, and how do they impact district productivity or learning? Within all organizations, including school districts, the *culture* is the way we do things, while the *climate* is the way any organization actually feels when you walk in the door or stay a while (Wilmore, 2002, 2004, 2007). What are the traditions, values, and mores that are utilized daily in our schools? What are the stories, the district lore? What are the district history and heritage? Who are the district heroes? All of this plays into defining the culture of the district as well as how it is perceived both internally and externally.

While some may wonder why organizational culture matters in districts and campuses, much research has been done by such notable names in educational leadership as Thomas Sergiovanni (1990, 1992, 1994, 1996, 2001, 2000), John Hoyle (2006), and, together, Lee Bolman and Terrence Deal (1997, 2006; Deal & Bolman, 2001), and others into the importance of organizational culture and climate and a supportive learning environment. Their work has been supplemented by that of Philip Schlechty (2001, 2005) into the intense need for supporting and sustaining educational innovation. Michael Fullan (2001, 2005) has been a leader in the call for sustained leadership and leading within a culture of change. Others have also entered the discussion regarding the importance of creating a positive school and district culture based on a focus on maximizing student learning and improving the learning community (Beaudoin & Taylor, 2004; Wilmore, 2002, 2004, 2007).

The ways in which a superintendent can address the development of a positive district culture are as different as the districts themselves. However, one thing all successful superintendents have in common is a sustained approach to improving and maintaining the culture that directly addresses the many facets of diversity within the district. They also focus on meeting the learning needs of every student. Integrating and incorporating diversity and different community cultures are important for making all people within the district feel valued and comfortable. The input from these different voices is critical in developing the district vision and determining specific ways of meeting targeted goals. To ask for input but then not use it makes people feel that their work and efforts are of little to no value. Therefore, ask for input and, as much as reasonably possible, include it in decision making, and let the providers know that you are doing exactly that. An educator friend once said that few things in the world are worse than making ordinary people feel ordinary. Appreciate and value diverse perspectives. Use them to help create a district culture and climate that maximize the learning opportunities for all students.

Providing an Effective Instructional Program

Having a well-developed vision, culture, and climate are not ends unto themselves. They are all pieces of the Big Puzzle in the Sky to help students learn. Another very important piece of this puzzle is providing an effective instructional program. If teachers are utilizing various teaching strategies but students are not learning, there is a problem. The goal of education is for all students to learn. Therefore, the goal of every teacher, every administrator, and every superintendent should be to help teachers teach so that students can understand the content being presented as well as how to use it in their lives. Sometimes, this means that instructional techniques teachers have used effectively for years are no longer meeting the needs of today's increasingly diverse and techno-savvy students. Although many teachers are open to change and innovation and are willing to get creative to help students learn, some wish that today's students were the same as yesterday's and that they could keep on teaching in the manner they have been teaching for years. It takes an insightful, sensitive, and supportive leadership team to promote, but not coerce, positive change.

It is important for all educators to be in sync with current demographics and needs. Now more than ever, everyone needs to be nurtured and mentored to enhance instructional techniques to meet the needs of today's students, rather than expecting the students to change their learning styles to meet a teacher's preferred teaching strategies. Sometimes, change will come with gnashing of teeth and slitting of wrists. Yet to effectively meet student needs, instructional change does need to occur.

Teachers are sometimes not going to change on their own. They look to their administrators at both the building and district levels to provide training in newly developed, research-based methodologies as well as the skills to analyze student data to find the relative strengths and weaknesses of various instructional techniques that might benefit each student. To provide this guidance, superintendents themselves must be able to utilize both qualitative and quantitative data, appropriate research methods, technology, and information systems to develop a long-range plan for the district that assesses the district's improvement and accountability systems. Further, the superintendent has to be able personally, or through the utilization of other administrators, to communicate this knowledge effectively, such that all educators can utilize the same sources of information and techniques to be of benefit inside classrooms. The bulk of the real teaching action is in the classrooms, so educators must have the most appropriate knowledge and skills to meet the instructional needs of students.

Superintendents themselves, as well as the school community, need to know how to use and promote the use of technology and information systems to enhance the district's curriculum and instruction, to monitor instructional practices, and to provide assistance to others who have needs for improvement. While the superintendent's job is not to do everything that takes place inside a district, the superintendent's role is to ensure that everything gets done. By displaying and utilizing up-to-date technologies, the superintendent models desirable behavior for the rest of the district. No one likes to hear from someone who is all talk but no action. By incorporating various forms of technology into daily life, a superintendent models this behavior for others. You do not need to be the one to host technology classes or to supervise all instruction going on in the district. However, you do need to ensure that someone is doing all of this and doing it very, very well. A former Navy admiral once said that what gets measured gets done. The same is true in assessing improvement in student learning through an enhanced instructional program. When everyone is held accountable for their responsibilities, more gets done.

While all of this may sound nice, if the district does not have the basic resources necessary for effective teaching and learning to take place, education will not be maximized. Therefore, we come back to the importance of effective communication skills for superintendents. The superintendent's job is to identify, allocate, and justify the resources necessary to develop and sustain an effective instructional program. The superintendent is the primary contact for all forms of resource and financial procurement from working with the school board and the school community to the legislature.

Applying Best Practices to Student Learning

To provide an effective instructional program, superintendents must lead the district in the application of best practices to enhance student learning. This is done in a number of ways. First, superintendents must have the ability to facilitate and engage in activities that use best practices and sound educational research to improve instructional programs. Again, this does not mean the superintendent must be inside classrooms teaching every day. It does mean that the superintendent has the knowledge and skills to be able to do so, if desired, and the ability to facilitate other district educators in doing likewise. Superintendents must be able to lead discussions inside the district itself as well as in the learning community on exactly what best practices are, why they are important, and how the district is utilizing them to improve student performance. The utilization of research-based data as cold hard facts when communicating with others enhances the superintendent's reputation as a true educational leader and someone who is current on what is going on in the field. In ways such as this, the superintendent assists schools and district personnel in understanding and applying research and best practices to improve student learning and, lest we forget, test scores.

Not every research-based technique or best practice works equally effectively with every student. This puts untold pressure on teachers who are trying to meet the diverse needs of so many different students in their classrooms at the same time. It can also lead to frustration and burnout for the same reasons. Superintendents need to understand, and let teachers know that they understand, how difficult the teaching job is. But understanding is not enough. Superintendents must understand and be able to apply human development theory and proven learning and motivational theories, while showing concern for the diversity of the learning process in place today. This can be done through the utilization of appropriate research strategies to profile student performance in the district as well as by analyzing differences among various district subgroups. These subgroups include, but are not limited to, age, race, gender, and socioeconomic status. When all of these strategies are utilized as a collective whole, the superintendent is maximizing best practices to provide and improve an effective instructional program.

Designing Comprehensive Professional Growth Plans

One difference between a pond and a lake may be the infiltration of oxygen through water flow. While most lakes have new water coming into them through moving currents, such as rivers, streams, and springs, often ponds do not. Ponds are created through the rise of ground water, without currents moving oxygen through them. Because of this, they sometimes develop algae. They sit there, stagnate, and can end up unappealing in appearance and smell.

As human beings, we are like lakes and ponds. If we do not have new knowledge and growth coming into us through currents of new research, best practices, professional associations, and trying out new instructional methodologies, we can become ponds that are not only stinky but also negatively affect our environment. But if we are on a continuing quest to be lifelong learners and constantly improve all facets of our lives, whether professional or personal, our districts can be like beautiful lakes, where fish and plants are living, growing, and thriving.

For this to occur, superintendents must have a solid knowledge of adult learning strategies. We must have the ability to apply technology and research to professional development designs that focus on authentic problems and tasks, have a significant mentoring and coaching element, and utilize conferencing and other techniques that promote new knowledge attainment and enhanced skills in the workplace. Superintendents must, therefore, have the ability to use strategies such as observations of others and collaborative reflection to help form comprehensive professional growth plans with district and school personnel, including themselves. A solid model for administrator development, which is also framed around the Educational Leadership Constituent Council Standards, is defined and explained in *Principal Induction: A Standards-Based Model for Administrator Development* (Wilmore, 2004). While originally designed for building-level principals, the model is equally effective for the professional development of all administrators, including superintendents.

All of us should be developing plans on how to make our lives as well as our careers better. As shown in Figure 3.2, the number one question in school leadership as well as life is, "How can I make this better?" When we stop genuinely reflecting and asking ourselves this question with regard to all facets of our lives, we stop growing, improving, and learning. We can become stale ponds. Do any of us really want to become a stale pond when we have so many opportunities available to become beautiful lakes, rivers, and streams that bring others joy and fulfillment? Being a lifelong learner means we have made a commitment to continue learning, changing, and evolving until we can be all we ever hope to be.

Figure 3.2   Improving the Process for Greater Student Achievement

Education = Making Their Lives Better

Source: Quincey & Kimberley Miller

PROBLEM-BASED LEARNING

Promoting a Positive District Culture:
Hello! I'm New Here!

Maggie Wall is the new superintendent of the Brandon Bend school district. She follows a superintendent who was not well liked or respected inside or outside the district. At the time of his departure, district morale was at an all-time low. While Maggie knows that most of the stories she has heard are either exaggerated or untrue, she still wants to learn from the previous situation and seeks to reclaim a positive district culture for Brandon Bend.

One of the most often repeated stories about her predecessor was that he was worse than unfriendly. He was always so sure that he was right, he sometimes came off as arrogant. Maggie knew that just being a "nice person" was not going to be enough to turn around the district climate. She knew that change was going to take a lot of work on her part as well as by others. This multifaceted endeavor would require all of her knowledge, skills, and experience.

Maggie began by putting together a personal strategic plan of things she intended to do inside and outside the district to refocus the entire learning community on the district vision. The school board that had hired her had convinced her that they were committed to improving teaching and learning and would stand behind her if things got tough. Maggie shared her plan for improving the district culture and climate with them. She sought their input on additional actions they could undertake together to enhance the district image as well as to refocus all stakeholders in putting their best attention into helping students from all segments of the community learn and be successful. Together, they created a plan to help accomplish this goal.

Maggie subsequently shared the ideas with all the district employees at a beginning of the year in-service meeting. She called it her "State of the District" address. In it, she outlined the school district vision and goals and the actions both she and the board planned to achieve the goals, and she asked them for their support. She also sought to open the formerly closed lines of communication by asking them to share any ideas they had to help turn the district around. In other words, Maggie sought to create open-door superintendency.

While firmly understanding that having this open door could create other problems, Maggie also believed that at this moment, generating trust between her and the rest of the district was of the utmost importance. As the school year began, Maggie put her plan into place as she had projected at the "State of the District" address. As time went by, she was on full alert to any signs of positive or negative reactions. She was in ongoing assessment mode to improve the district's culture and climate continuously for the benefit of teaching and learning.

Reflective Practice: Pause and Think

Through the use of reflection and higher-order thinking skills:

1. What other methods of district culture assessment could Maggie have utilized before developing her plan to improve it?

2. Was it a good idea to involve the school board in her plans? Why, or why not?

3. Was doing a "State of the District" address to all employees the best approach she could have taken? Why, or why not?

4. Discuss both the positives and potential negatives of Maggie making a public statement regarding her "open door."

5. Discuss the concept of people working their way upward to Maggie's office with concerns via a "chain-of-command" philosophy. How could Maggie make sure that every person upset over some tiny thing does not show up in her office without hearing her own words of "open door" thrown back at her?

6. What other strategies could Maggie have included in her plan to handle open communication issues?

Providing an Effective Instructional Program: But We're Doing the Best That We Can!

Superintendent Jandie Carroll has just returned from the American Association of School Administrators National Conference on Education. While there, she attended several sessions that focused on instructional alignment to district and campus goals as well as to state-mandated testing standards. She, as well as her superintendent friends, is always looking for ways to improve student performance as measured by these high-stakes tests. The idea of alignment was presented in these sessions differently from the way she had thought about it in the past. Jandie likes what she has learned and looks forward to researching more about it.

Upon returning home, Jandie worked with her curriculum directors to study the issue of curriculum and instruction alignment. She discovered that while her curriculum directors were working very hard on this issue, they had not been doing so from a perspective of tying instruction to specific standards. Nor had they considered doing a curriculum audit to determine if their materials were, in fact, truly addressing every piece of every standard, rather than just assuming that they were because the teachers really were, indeed, working hard.

Jandie, with the help of the curriculum directors, principals, and many teachers, took on the task of conducting a major district curriculum audit. This process took quite a long time, as the instruments by which to audit the curriculum had to be developed. Then, it took even more time to conduct the audit, analyze the results, and make recommendations on how to provide a more effective instructional program. All together, the process took most of the academic year.

Based on the results of this research and data-driven process, many changes were made within the curriculum itself and in its delivery. Some were minor edits. Others were more far-reaching and in-depth. Some people felt the changes were a slap at their experience and creditability as educators. Time was spent talking to all teachers about the process and how it could result in helping them teach smarter rather than teaching harder. In the end, changes were made to both the district's curriculum and instruction that resulted in a more aligned framework from which to teach.

Reflective Practice: Pause and Think

1. What exactly is a curriculum audit? What elements should be included in the development of a curriculum audit?

2. Should curriculum and instruction be aligned with district goals and test standards? Why, or why not?

3. Discuss the issues involved with "teaching to the test" in regard to aligning curriculum, instruction, and assessment.

4. What types of people should be involved in the development, implementation, and assessment of a curriculum audit?

5. Develop a proposed model and time line of how you could potentially facilitate the alignment of curriculum and instruction to your district goals and standards as your district responds to No Child Left Behind.

6. How could your district's curriculum development process be improved? What role could you play in that process?

7. Once a curriculum audit and subsequent changes have been put into place and implemented for a period of time, how would you assess the process and its results for improved teaching and learning?

Applying Best Practices to Student Learning: Addressing the Dropout Problem in an Urban District

As superintendent of a large urban school district, Dr. Paul Meyer was disturbed that district efforts to stem the dropout rate were having negligible impact. Over a period of time, the district had opened several "alternative" middle and high schools. Although they were experiencing some success, far too many students, particularly those from the district's large lower socioeconomic population, still were not attending and, thus, not learning or being served. Dr. Meyer found this statistic unacceptable and began an in-depth district-wide needs analysis to accumulate and study as much data as possible on why students were not in attendance at any school. He worked with his school board and administrative team to put together a blue-ribbon panel of district and city people to work on the project. He wanted all facets of the area to be represented. He made sure the panel consisted of people from different walks of life and went beyond educators and parents, including local businesses that were hiring many of the dropouts, social service agency representatives, people from diverse racial and cultural groups, two city council members, and citizens who may or may not have students in school at the time. His effort to get such a widespread representation on the panel brought different voices with diverse perspectives together at the same time to address a problem that was impacting the district as well as the city and society as a whole as students ended their educations prematurely.

Through time, research, and great effort, the panel identified several key reasons why the current structure for keeping at-risk students in school was not as successful as desired. They further studied adolescent learning theory and current research-based best practices to meet the needs of the targeted populations. As a result, the blue-ribbon panel eventually made a formal proposal to Dr. Meyer, which constituted a virtual restructuring of not only the district's alternative programs but also mainstream programs within both the elementary and secondary schools. These programs were designed to keep students actively engaged and to provide learning that was directly applicable to their interests and needs in the work environment. Dr. Meyer studied the panel's thorough proposal, which included a projected budget and time line for implementation. After some modifications to the plan were made, he eventually presented it to the school board. They approved it with great respect and appreciation for the community and district personnel who had put such obvious effort and concern into it. Eventually, the proposed restructuring was put into place a segment at a time. Through the utilization of community-based support, research of student needs, and the application of best practices, the district was better able to meet the needs of all students in a supportive learning environment.

Reflective Practice: Pause and Think

1. Define and describe exactly what "best practices" are and why they are important in optimizing student learning.

2. Discuss age and developmentally appropriate instructional strategies and their implications for student success.

3. Why did Dr. Meyer go to the trouble of creating such a diversified blue-ribbon panel to address an educational issue? Why didn't he focus on the solution with existing personnel rather than utilizing community members who might not have training in best practices?

4. What other interventions could Dr. Meyer have utilized to address the dropout problem?

5. Design an articulation plan the district could utilize prior to implementating the new programs that would also involve multiple district and city constituencies.

6. Describe an assessment model with a time line that would address a new program's learning and cost-effectiveness. How could these things be measured?

Designing Comprehensive Professional Growth Plans: The Sowell-Watson CSD University

The Sowell-Watson Consolidated School District (CSD) consists of approximately 35 square miles combined from the former Sowell and Watson school districts. The districts merged during the past two years to save costs and offer additional courses, particularly on the Advanced Placement level, to their relatively small student populations. Although there have been some glitches in the consolidation process, by and large, the combination of the two districts has gone well.

Great planning has gone into the merger of students, personnel, facilities, and other resources. The former superintendent of Sowell decided to retire but continues to serve as a consultant to the newly combined district. The superintendent of Watson, Gary Mark Carter, is now leading the newly merged district. Again, due to excellent long-term strategic planning and the development, articulation, and implementation of a joint vision, the consolidated district is doing well.

As the initial transition and original issues surrounding it fade into the past, Gary Mark is looking to the future on ways to enhance teaching and learning. One strategy he would like to implement is to ask each educator, including himself and other administrators, to develop, implement, and assess their own professional growth and development. Working with staff and campuses, Gary Mark convinced the school board to put time, resources, and training into helping each educator identify personal strengths and weaknesses. The goal would then be for each person to use this data to create personal improvement strategies.

The prospect of every educator having a professional development plan has caused some concerns in Watson-Sowell. Some older educators resented the implication that they needed to improve. Other educators felt that they had never had to do a development plan in the past when the districts were separate, so why should they have to do one now? Some teachers said, "Whatever. This is just the newest bandwagon idea administration has come up with. Ignore it. It will go away soon enough." All in all, the whole idea was not received favorably, and Gary Mark had considerable difficulty turning around this negative perception.

Being a persistent and proactive superintendent, Gary Mark did not want to give up on the concept. While he realized that he might have done a better job articulating the vision such that people could understand its purpose better, he also realized that was water under the bridge now. "So," he wondered, "what am I going to do now?"

At his next administrators' meeting, Gary Mark put the whole idea on the table and asked for input from their perspectives. Different people brought up different ideas. All of the ideas centered on turning the negative perception into a positive one. For several weeks, into the spring semester, the administrative team worked on different ideas. But not one of them seemed perfect. None seemed like anything that could generate excitement and inspiration within the faculty, principals, etc. about improving teaching and leadership skills.

As time progressed, attention wavered from the idea as stress over high-stakes state testing moved to the forefront of everyone's minds. Virtually everyone was stressed out. Teachers were stressed. Administrators and staff were stressed. Students and parents were very stressed. Even Gary Mark was stressed! The idea of professional development plans fell to the bottom of his Most Pressing Needs list.

One day, as the principals and administrators showed up, tired and weary, for their regular meeting with Gary Mark, someone jokingly said that what they all needed was some stress relief. In fact, the entire district could benefit from some fun. Everyone agreed. The administrators began brainstorming what could be done that would be uplifting to the teachers and still provide good stewardship of the district vision.

Although some ideas were completely absurd, some were not bad at all. Eventually an idea emerged about having a big district "event" where faculty and staff could participate in different concurrent activities that centered on teaching, learning, best practices, and, especially, on promoting a better district culture and climate than everyone was experiencing at the moment. Somehow in the discussion, someone came up with the idea of having a Watson-Sowell CSD University. They could use different district facilities as "university campuses." Each campus would come up with its own theme for professional development activities and would also give away free "university campus" T-shirts, etc. to participants. Planners were encouraged to be as creative as possible. The criteria were that the activities must be research based, worthwhile, of benefit to those who chose them, and—absolutely—fun.

Before making a decision, each principal brought the idea to their campuses to get faculty and staff input. Although some originally thought that the idea of doing anything extra was absurd at that time of the year, others bought into it completely. Nothing spreads enthusiasm like enthusiasm, and few things generate enthusiasm as much as creativity. To help motivate people, the district provided prizes for the most resourceful and worthwhile activities offered on each university campus. Everyone got to pick the activities in which they wished to participate. Plenty of free food was provided, and "diplomas" were given at the end of the day. Teachers relieved stress and learned helpful new best practices. While certainly this was not a day centered on writing a professional development plan, the faculty and staff were eased into the idea of individual selection based on their own professional needs. Gary Mark and his team hoped the Watson-Sowell CSD University would be an initial positive step in moving the district toward individual accountability and professional development.

Reflective Practice: Pause and Think

1. Create a model of professional development themes that could occur on a minimum of five "university campuses."

2. Develop a minimum of five engaging professional development activities that could occur on one of the selected themed university campuses you generated above.

3. In what ways could, or could not, the idea of a district university lead teachers into being more receptive to individual professional development plans?

4. Is it realistic to expect professional development to be engaging? Why, or why not? Support your response.

5. How could a project such as this be evaluated? What types of data should be included in the assessment?

6. What else could be done to help ease teachers and other educators into being comfortable with professional development plans rather than seeing them as a negative or punitive assignment?

ASSESSMENT MODEL

Standard 2: A school district leader who has the knowledge and ability to promote the success of all students by promoting a positive school culture, providing an effective instructional program, applying best practices to student learning, and designing comprehensive professional growth plans for staff

In Table 3.1, you will find a planning rubric for assessing your progress toward this standard. Vertical and horizontal mentoring are important elements in maximizing your success. For additional reading on administrator induction and mentoring, see *Principal Induction: A Standards-Based Model for Administrator Development* (Wilmore, 2004).

Table 3.1   Planning Rubric for Standard 2

Element	Goals to Meet Standard for Improved School District Leadership	Specific Activities Designed to Achieve Standard	People and Resources Needed to Operationalize This Strategy	Date by Which Activity Will Be Completed	Evidence of Standard Attainment
2.1 Promote Positive School Culture	a. Develop a sustained approach to improve and maintain a positive district culture for learning that capitalizes on multiple aspects of diversity to meet the learning needs of all students.				
2.2 Provide Effective Instructional Program	a. Demonstrate an understanding of a variety of instructional research methodologies and be able to analyze the comparable strengths and weaknesses of each method.				
	b. Be able to use qualitative and quantitative data, appropriate research methods, technology, and information systems to develop a long-range plan for a district that assesses the district's improvement and accountability systems.				
	c. Demonstrate the ability to use and promote technology and information systems to enrich district curriculum and instruction, monitor instructional practices, and provide assistance to administrators who have needs for improvement.				
	d. Demonstrate the ability to allocate and justify resources to sustain the instructional program.				

2.3 Apply Best Practices to Student Learning	a. Demonstrate the ability to facilitate and engage in activities that use best practices and sound educational research to improve instructional programs.						
	b. Demonstrate an ability to assist school and district personnel in understanding and applying best practices for student learning.						
	c. Understand and be able to apply human development theory, proven learning and motivational theories, and concern for diversity to the learning process.						
	d. Understand how to use appropriate research strategies to profile student performance in a district and analyze differences among subgroups.						
2.4 Design Comprehensive Professional Growth Plans	a. Demonstrate knowledge of adult learning strategies and the ability to apply technology and research to professional development design, focusing on authentic problems and tasks, mentoring, coaching, conferencing, and other techniques that promote new knowledge and skills in the workplace.						
	b. Demonstrate the ability to use strategies such as observations and collaborative reflection to help form comprehensive professional growth plans with district and school personnel.						
	c. Develop personal professional growth plans that reflect commitment to life-long learning and best practices.						

Ways for You to Do It:

A superintendent leader can enhance systematic school improvement by using the following strategies:

- Providing staff development that is centered on teacher and student needs
- Focusing on quality staff development rather than quantity of opportunities provided.
- Soliciting and valuing campus opinions on curriculum, hiring, staff development, and budgeting
- Being seen on campuses often. Periodically teach a lesson on different grade or content areas. It will help keep you human and tied to the "real world."
- Through the utilization of committees with significant teacher input, developing a uniform district curriculum that is not totally focused on standardized testing, but addresses the holistic needs of each student.
- Actively seeking to improve the performance of every student through tailoring curriculum and instruction to a wide range of abilities, goals, and other campus qualities
- Developing, implementing, evaluating, and refining an induction and mentoring program for new educators, experienced educators in new roles, and any who need assistance
- Improving or removing ineffective teachers and administrators
- Supporting consistent, firm discipline as outlined in a collaboratively developed Discipline Management Plan that is clearly articulated to the school community
- Implementing an effective communication system among all district campuses and departments
- Encouraging the utilization of campus and district creativity in providing time for educators to meet and plan with their peers
- Being creative in scheduling meeting times; Always having planning meetings after school does not maximize employee physical, intellectual, or emotional productivity.
- As much as is reasonably possible provide small class sizes to minimize the teacher-to-student ratio particularly with students who are experiencing learning difficulties.

CONCLUSIONS

School districts, as well as campuses themselves, are changing in front of our very eyes. Instructional strategies and methodologies that worked in the past may no longer be effective. Today superintendents must forge forward in advocating, nurturing, and sustaining an enhanced instructional program that focuses on student learning and the professional development of all of those who impact student learning. This, of course, includes us. We, too, should be learning and growing at all times. An excellent tool for achieving this is through the development and utilization of professional development plans for all educators. These may vary in different ways, but the one thing they will all have in common is their commitment to proactive, accountable growth. The utilization of mentoring is truly encouraged for all involved as is conferencing, the utilization of data in planning, developing, and utilizing the plan, and the use of conferencing and committed reflective practice in its implementation.

Superintendents have an important role in the district's culture and climate, which are strong elements in the success of any organization. Being an overt action player in meeting the needs of all forms of diversity within the district starts at the top and is critically important to those watching us every day. The superintendent's commitment to a multiplicity of cultures and learning styles will have a strong positive impact on the rest of the district. Remember, what others see you value and do will be strongly correlated to what others value and do. Therefore, it is up to us to provide an effective instructional program that utilizes best practices to enhance learning critical to student, campus, district, and societal success.

The Ultimate Application

The following questions are designed to assist you in applying higher-level thinking skills through application. Either alone, or in a group setting, respond to each question based upon your own knowledge, experience, and further research.

1. Create and describe an ideal learning environment scenario in which the superintendent advocates, nurtures, and sustains a district culture and instructional program that is conducive to student learning and staff professional growth.

2. Discuss the issue of superintendents involving others in the district as a part of shared decision making. Who should be included, who should not, and why? Synthesize the concepts, draw conclusions, and create possible applications for each.

3. Describe the attributes of organizational culture of a district you are aware of. It does not need to be your own. Compare and contrast the culture of that district with an ideal situation. Draw conclusions and implications for district leadership.

4. Design a plan of specific ways that you as the district's top instructional leader can enhance student performance. Include a projected time line and model of assessment.

5. Explain why it is important for superintendents to join professional organizations, participate in organizational meetings, conferences, and activities, and to read professional journals. What would you say to a superintendent who claimed not to have time to do these things?

6. Explain the benefits of superintendents encouraging other administrators and teachers to participate in professional growth activities and creative ways to provide funding for their support.

7. Describe the benefits of action research for active district improvement. Outline a project you would like to see happen within your district. Describe the purposes, steps, assessments, necessary resources, potential outcomes, and implications it would have for improved student learning.

8. How can a superintendent as CEO of a school district manage to advocate, nurture, and sustain a district culture that promotes maximized student learning?

Leadership Through Management of District Organization, Operations, and Resources

"Outstanding leaders go out of the way to boost the self-esteem of their personnel. If people believe in themselves it's amazing what they can accomplish."

—Sam Walton

> **Standard 3:** A school district leader who has the knowledge and ability to promote the success of all students by managing the organization, operations, and resources in a way that promotes a safe, efficient, and effective learning environment

INTRODUCTION

Leading and managing a school district is somewhat like working a jigsaw puzzle. Everything has to fit together perfectly, or the puzzle won't work out. You may think you have the right puzzle piece in the right place and then find out, "Oops! It won't fit!" Then you have to start looking all over again to find where the piece goes while simultaneously continuing to look for a different piece that is supposed to go where you originally thought that this one went. It can get confusing.

Isn't that just like school district leadership? About the time that you think you have one problem solved, another one pops up. Sometimes problems are leadership issues that look to the future and relate to the district vision. At other times, they are management issues that have to do with the daily functions of the district. Standard 3 focuses primarily on management issues. It is most concerned with the management oversight of the "organization, operations, and resources" of the district such that there is a "safe, efficient, and effective learning environment." In other words, the superintendent is responsible for ensuring that the organization runs smoothly so everyone can do their jobs efficiently and effectively. When the air-conditioning goes out on hot days, the learning environment is impacted. When the plumbing backs up, the learning environment is definitely affected. And if someone is pointing a gun inside a campus, the learning environment is more than impacted. So while the other standards concentrate on various academic issues, let us not forget that for students to maximize their learning potential, every piece of the puzzle has to fit perfectly, and amazingly, all must fit at the same time.

Figure 4.1 shows the critical elements that standards-based research utilizes in leadership through management.

Figure 4.1   Standards-Based Superintendents as Managers

Standards-Based Superintendents Are Good Managers As Well As Leaders

- Organization of the district.
- District operations.
- District resources.

Source: Photo taken by Elizabeth Hall

PHILOSOPHICAL FRAMEWORK

Managing the Organization of the District

There are so many ways in which superintendents daily manage the organization of the district. One of the most important is systems thinking, whereby each component of the global "system" is treated as a combined gestalt of individual components and how they interact and impact each other for the best outcomes (Fullan, 2005; Hoyle et al., 2005). For each of these things to occur the superintendent must have a sound working knowledge of research that can be used to enhance the learning of students, their development as holistic human beings, the organizational development of the district per se, how teachers teach, and the management of data to maximize the learning of each of the district's diverse students.

Superintendents can do this by displaying effective organization of the fiscal, human, and material resources of the district in such a way that top priority is always given to student learning and safety. This is done through the utilization of sound district budgeting processes, carrying out fiduciary responsibilities, and ensuring that financial and human resources are utilized in ways that student achievement is always of the utmost importance in decision making.

In performing their daily organizational responsibilities, superintendents are expected to design and implement district planning and evaluation based on criteria that include student and campus equity, effectiveness, and efficiency. All of this is based on the application of legal principles that promote educational equity for everyone and is done in safe, efficient, and effective facilities.

For any of these things to be accomplished, a superintendent needs to be able to manage time effectively. Remember, it may or may not be the role of the superintendent to do all of these things personally. However, it is always part of the superintendent's role to facilitate their getting done efficiently and effectively.

Managing District Operations

Managing the operations of the district depends, in large part, on the superintendent having excellent communication skills. In this top leadership position, articulating the district vision through the management of daily operations and so that others can understand it is critical to success. As in the development of the vision, all stakeholders have a need to know and understand what is taking place; why it is taking place; what their roles and responsibilities are; and how the entire process will be assessed, modified, and improved. This is why it is important for superintendents, other district-level administrators, and principals actively to involve as many varied stakeholders as possible in planning processes. Again, people support what they help create. Community collaboration and getting the input of as many district personnel as reasonably possible is important to the success of all new ideas.

Actual communication plans, or articulation plans, of whatever has been planned are then put into place for integrating all of the district's schools and divisions such that everyone knows what is going on and why. As shown in Figure 4.2, this can be done through the involvement of multiple stakeholders in aligning district resources and priorities to maximize stakeholder ownership and accountability.

As in the initial development and alignment of district and campus goals to facilitate the vision, the budgeting and purchasing of resources must be prioritized and directly aligned with specific district goals and objectives. Just as there should be no "sacred cows" in curriculum or other academic programming, we also should not continue to purchase things that we have always bought in the past when we may not need them anymore or something else can achieve the same objective better. How can we

Figure 4.2   Multiple Stakeholders Help Prioritize and Align Resources With Needs

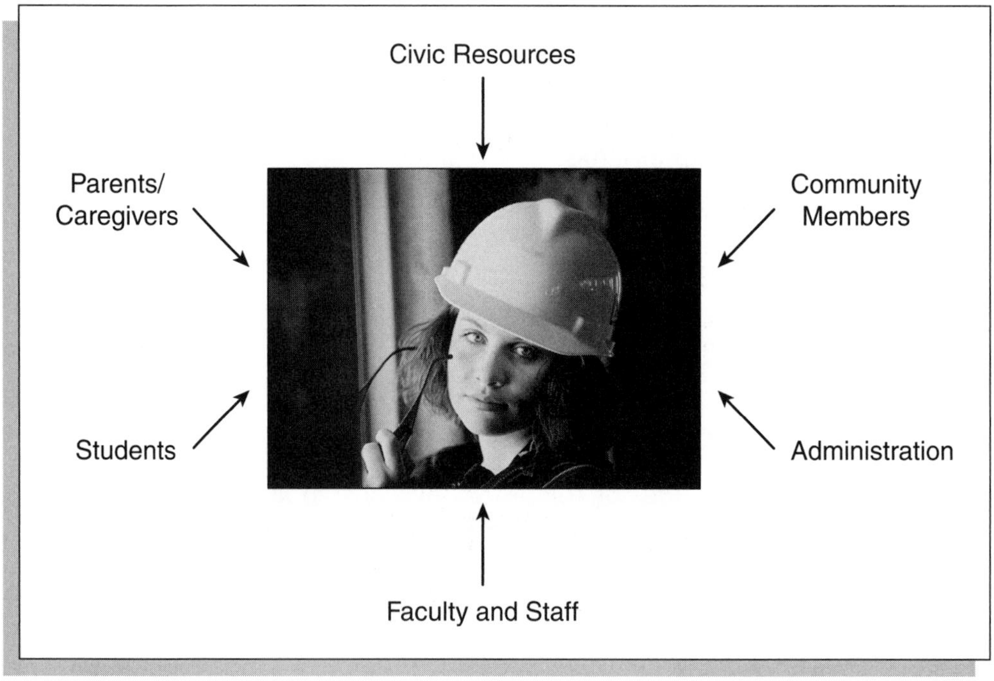

Source: Kee Badders

maximize the utilization of what is purchased to directly target district goals and priorities? As shown in Figures 4.3, 4.4, 4.5, and 4.6, the superintendent leads the district in quantitatively and qualitatively asking these questions in response to budget development and implementation:

- Are our goals directly aligned with our vision to meet the needs of our students?
- Is our budget aligned with our goals?
- How are we measuring our success in reaching district goals while maintaining cost-effectiveness?
- Are there better ways we can achieve the same objectives?

Superintendents can utilize various forms and styles of research to answer these questions. These include using appropriate and effective needs assessments, research-based data, and various group-processing skills to build consensus, communicate with the school community, and resolve conflicts to align district resources with the district vision. Figure 4.7 gives a visual description of aligning district resources with the vision, then measuring their effectiveness.

Figure 4.3   Are Our Goals Directly Aligned With Our Vision to Meet the Needs of Students?

Source: Photo courtesy of David Quisenberry Photography

Figure 4.4   Is Our Budget Aligned With Our Goals?

Source: Photo taken by Elizabeth Hall

Figure 4.5   How Are We Measuring Our Success in Reaching District Goals While Maintaining Cost-Effectiveness?

Source: Michael & Karen Fawcett

Figure 4.6   Are There Better Ways We Can Achieve the Same Objectives?

Source: Courtesy of Lee, Alison, & Elizabeth Hefley

Figure 4.7   Strategic Planning

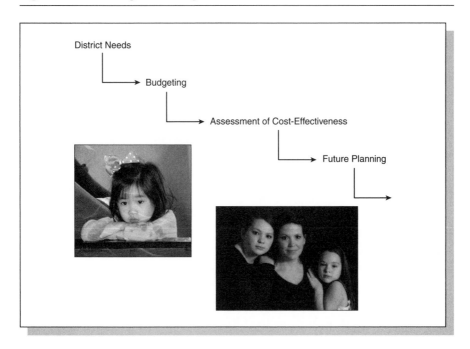

Source: Photo courtesy of David Quisenberry Photography

Consequently, planning, communicating, implementing, assessing, and making modifications based on data-driven assessments becomes an ongoing cyclical process that never ends. District and campus improvement should also never end. There is always room for improvement, always another student in need, and always a search for the best strategies to reach the ideal situation. This ideal situation is the vision of the district.

Managing District Resources

Referring back to Figures 4.1, 4.2, and 4.7, the process for managing the organization and operation of the district is an ongoing one. A key element is the management of district resources in ways that maximize cost effectiveness. This is done with a goal of providing, in essence, the most "bang for the buck" in producing increased student learning. Superintendents daily use various problem-solving skills; their knowledge of strategic, long-range, and operational planning; and technology to achieve these goals. Superintendents make effective, legal, and equitable use of fiscal, human, and material resource allocation that focuses on improving teaching and learning. To do this effectively, superintendents are constantly in search of new, creative, and alternative ways to provide additional resources to facilitate student learning and achievement of the vision. If we cannot fund something in one way, how else can we achieve the same goals through alternative means?

In so doing, superintendents apply an understanding of district financial structures and models to ensure that adequate resources are allocated equitably within the district such that the needs of all students are met. Districts must utilize strong financial structures that include regular audits of funds from both internal and external sources, including from the local, state, and federal government levels. One way to make sure this happens is through the utilization of current technologies for all forms of fiduciary management, business procedures, and scheduling.

The public has a right to know how tax dollars are spent. Citizens can create havoc in your life if they do not feel district resources are being utilized appropriately. Through including multiple stakeholders from diverse areas of the district in the decision-making process as well as having and using a clear communication network, superintendents can save themselves and others a lot of grief. Someone will always be out there asking questions. It is best to be proactive by having clear mechanisms and structures in place whereby all questions can be answered truthfully, honestly, and in a manner that Average Joe Citizen can understand, even when he does not want to understand.

PROBLEM-BASED LEARNING

Managing the Organization of the District: A Winding Road in an Urban Area

When Jill Jones became superintendent of a large, urban, diverse school district, she was very excited. Having been successful in each of her previous superintendent roles, she had now reached a goal for which she had worked a very long time: to lead a big district in a metropolitan area. She had worked with diverse groups successfully in the past and was greatly looking forward to working in the Lanier Dyson district with its multiple racial and cultural student groups.

When Jill arrived to begin work, she met a positive reception from everyone. Her intelligence, sunny disposition, and caring attitude won her immediate new relationships and friendships. As time went by and Jill settled into her job, however, the excitement of her new role gave way to the reality of doing what was best for so many different subgroups, each vying with different needs, sometimes at the expense of each other. Eventually, Jill knew she was going to have to make some tough decisions relating to district priorities, the vision, goals, and instructional and extracurricular leadership as they related to funding. Lanier Dyson might be a large district with a sizeable budget, but it also had large needs and did not have the money to fund everyone's desires.

The more Jill dug into the recent history of the district, the more she learned that no cohesive, overriding vision connected each segment toward common goals. She knew immediately that she would have to address this problem right away. Money was being spent for worthwhile things, but expenditures did not seem aligned toward specific goals. Project expenditures, even large ones, seemed haphazard and based upon making different subgroups happy. Yet when Jill questioned some of the previous budget line items, she quickly learned that certain things were always budgeted due to various "pet projects" of people both inside and outside the district. In other words, some things were done for political purposes and to keep the peace in the district.

This concerned Jill very much. She was determined that everything the district did should be fair and equitable to meet the needs of today's students. On the other hand, still being relatively new, she did not want to irritate people she was just getting to know. "Where is the research to help me through this?" she thought. "It really is a winding road to achieve the vision of an urban area where everyone has different wants, needs, and desires and options of how to achieve them."

Reflective Practice: Pause and Think

Through the use of reflection and higher-order thinking skills, respond to the following questions:

1. If you were Jill, what would you do *first?*

2. Create a model for a large urban district to develop a common vision when none is in place. Include components to address educational equity across the district. Be specific.

3. Based upon organizational leadership theory and research-based knowledge of student learning processes, develop a plan by which Jill can lead Lanier Dyson into a more mature organizational leadership culture and climate while also maximizing student and teacher productivity.

4. Jill is concerned about angering people whom she is just getting to know. How can she address potential conflict while still maintaining integrity and professionalism?

5. In what ways can district data management and technology be utilized to help Jill achieve her goals?

6. Define and explain indicators of equity, effectiveness, and efficiency that can be used to measure district performance in meeting the needs of all students.

Managing District Operations: Baby, It's Raining Outside!

As superintendent of the Wimberley Public Schools, Frank Redding is in what some would say a great position. But others say, "Think again." Due to unexpected revenue resulting from oil leases on district property, the district has come into a large lump sum payment that has not been budgeted. Although additional monies might come from the oil leases in the future, no one knows for sure when, if, or how much they will be. Therefore, the district is trying to exercise prudent financial planning with regard to utilizing this lump sum payment. Because the district receiving of this money has made big news in the community, many people have their own ideas of how to use it. Ten of the most vocalized and popular ideas are, in no particular order:

1. Reduce taxes.

2. Give teachers a raise.

3. Build a new football stadium and weight-training facility.

4. Expand the fine arts department.

5. Renovate and update computer labs and technology on all campuses.

6. Restore elementary music, art, and physical education classes that were eliminated by previous budget cuts.

7. Divide the lump sum into equitable segments and allow each campus and department to set its own priorities for how to spend its share.

8. Open a child care center for employees who have preschool children.

9. Build a district professional development center and name it for the oil company that supplied the money.

10. Invest the funds. Save them, and the interest they earn, for a rainy day.

Everywhere Frank goes around town, people have their own ideas of how to use the money. He knows that whatever he recommends to the school board, some groups will be unhappy.

Reflective Practice: Pause and Think

1. What is Frank's actual role in determining how, or if, this money should be spent?

2. What is the role of the school board in regard to the same issues?

3. Develop a consensus-building model by which this district can reach a tenable agreement on how to utilize the funds. Provide examples.

4. Look at the 10 most popular ideas of how to use the money described above. Compare and contrast the pros and cons of each suggestion.

5. If it was up to you, which of the 10 ideas would you choose? Why?

6. What additional ideas could the district use to maximize the money's impact for long-term productivity?

Managing District Resources: Lord, Please Don't Let Me Be Misunderstood

Landon Cole has been superintendent of Merciful Springs school district for the last 10 years. During this time, the district has experienced phenomenal suburban growth. During the last seven years, four new schools have been built and opened. Although their construction has had some impact on the district tax rate, it has been held to a minimum due in large part to increased property values within the district.

One of the reasons for the growth has been the construction and opening of a large power plant located outside the city limit but inside the school district lines. The power plant has not paid city taxes but has paid county and school district taxes. These funds have also played a factor in the construction and staffing of the new schools. Many of the families moving into the district have one or more persons employed at the power plant, so its presence has been of primary importance to the district, both in terms of financial support and in terms of imposing the academic responsibility of providing an excellent education to the children of the workers and everyone else.

In the past year, rumors circulated that the power plant might close due to laws deregulating the energy industry. This rumor caused a good deal of concern, as people wondered if they would lose their jobs or have to move. As superintendent, Landon sought to be proactive. He worked consistently and collaboratively with power plant management and regulators so he could conduct as much long-term planning as possible for the potential impact this closure could have on the district.

In late spring, everyone's worst fears became real. The power plant announced it would close the following September. As expected, some employees will be transferred, thus leaving the town and school district. This will impact the number of students enrolled in the district. Other employees will simply be let go. While they would be given a severance package, it will not be enough to sustain their families indefinitely. Some are staying and looking for different jobs, while others are moving in search of greener fields elsewhere. This change will also have an impact on small businesses in the community, which depend on the power point employees' commerce for survival.

In short, the town and the school district are in for some major changes. Landon is thankful he has been looking to the future and trying to minimize the impact of the power plant closure in case it happened. However, there are still grave concerns. The district will lose students. The district will also lose some teachers and support staff who will move away with spouses. Landon and the school board, which will now have two vacancies due to trustees moving away, realize this transition period will be traumatizing for many people. They want to minimize this effect. They are also concerned that they may need to close at least one school due to decreased enrollment. The choice of which one it will be, especially because several campuses are still new, will be a difficult decision.

Teachers and staff will likely have to be reassigned. District attendance zones will likely have to be redrawn. Landon, his staff, and the board know they have a long spring and summer in front of them. They earnestly hope to involve as much of the community as possible as hard decisions are made. Their goal is to make this transition as easy as possible, but they realize that is difficult when people's livelihoods are on the line.

Reflective Practice: Pause and Think

1. What should Landon do *first* after hearing this announcement? Why?

2. What types of data must Landon, other administrators, and the board utilize in decision making regarding the financial impact of the closing on the district? Be specific.

3. Brainstorm ways the district could minimize this financial impact.

4. If it is determined that a campus should close, what data should be used in the decision-making process to determine which one it should be?

5. In such a period of disarray, what issues should Landon keep on the forefront of his mind in relation to equity for all remaining students and employees?

6. Because two board members are moving, there will be two board vacancies before the next board election. What process should be utilized to fill them? A called election? Board appointments? Other? Explain and support your response and define the factors that must be considered.

ASSESSMENT MODEL

> **Standard 3:** A school district leader who has the knowledge and ability to promote the success of all students by managing the organization, operations, and resources in a way that promotes a safe, efficient, and effective learning environment

In Table 4.1, you will find a planning rubric for assessing your progress toward this standard. Vertical and horizontal mentoring are important elements in maximizing your success. For additional reading on administrator induction and mentoring, see *Principal Induction: A Standards-Based Model for Administrator Development* (Wilmore, 2004).

Table 4.1 Planning Rubric for Standard 3

Element	Goals to Meet Standard for Improved School District Leadership	Specific Activities Designed to Achieve Standard	People and Resources Needed to Operationalize This Strategy	Date by Which Activity Will Be Completed	Evidence of Standard Attainment
3.1 Manage the Organization	a. Demonstrate the ability to use research-based knowledge of learning, teaching, student development, organizational development, and data management to optimize learning for all students.				
	b. Demonstrate effective organization of fiscal, human, and material resources, giving priority to student learning and safety, and demonstrate an understanding of district budgeting processes and fiduciary responsibilities.				
	c. Demonstrate an ability to manage time effectively and to deploy financial and human resources in a way that promotes student achievement.				
	d. Demonstrate the ability to organize district-based indicators of equity, effectiveness, and efficiency and be able to apply legal principles that promote educational equity.				
	e. Demonstrate an understanding of how to apply legal principles to promote educational equity and provide safe, effective, and efficient facilities.				

3.2 Manage Operations	a. Demonstrate the ability to involve stakeholders in aligning resources and priorities to maximize ownership and accountability.					
	b. Use appropriate and effective needs assessment, research-based data, and group process skills to build consensus, communicate, and resolve conflicts to align resources with the district vision.					
	c. Develop staff communication plans for integrating the district's schools and divisions.					
	d. Develop a plan to promote and support community collaboration among district personnel.					
3.3 Manage Resources	a. Use problem-solving skills and knowledge of strategic, long-range, and operational planning (including applications of technology) in the effective, legal, and equitable use of fiscal, human, and material resource allocation that focuses on teaching and learning.					
	b. Creatively seek new resources to facilitate learning.					
	c. Apply an understanding of school district finance structures and models to ensure that adequate financial resources are allocated equitably for the district. Apply and assess current technologies for management, business procedures, and scheduling.					

Ways for You to Do It:

A superintendent leader can enhance systematic school improvement by the following strategies:

- Ensuring all district facilities look their best and keeping up with renovations, repairs, and upgrades, including technology
- Utilizing teachers and others "in the trenches" in budgeting decision making
- Visiting campuses regularly to have firsthand knowledge of needed resources
- Prioritizing budgeting so that expenditures focus on the greatest student needs first
- Utilizing effective budget planning, communication, and adoption by the school board such that books, equipment, and other supplies can be purchased and arrive by the first day of school
- Being financially prudent and astute: if a potential expenditure does not pass the "smell test," do not buy it.
- Closely supervising those who handle money on the campuses, through athletics and the arts, at the district office, and elsewhere
- Having all audits conducted by appropriately credentialed accountants in a timely and efficient manner
- As much as possible, improving employee pay, benefits, and retirement
- Maximizing staff, teacher, and administrator placements to maximize student learning
- Developing, articulating, implementing, and evaluating a fair building use policy for entities outside the school that wish to utilize district facilities
- Soliciting as much community involvement as reasonably possible
- Actively working to develop collaborative partnerships with local businesses, service groups, and others with a common mission of helping students succeed

CONCLUSIONS

It is necessary and wonderful for all districts to have visionary leaders as superintendents. However, it is also necessary and equally wonderful to have superintendents who can organize and manage the district's operations and resources. If a district does not have a leader who can proactively manage the daily operations of the district, align the district resources and operations with the collaboratively developed vision and goals, communicate everything to everyone, and manage to hold the walls of the schools together on a daily basis, the district will be headed for trouble. So while we emphasize the leadership of the district, it is also imperative that we not forget the critically important management of the district. Without a superintendent who can efficiently and effectively provide a safe learning environment through good organization, appropriate management of operations, and alignment of district resources with the vision and goals, it is very difficult for the district to move forward in a timely and successful manner. "Pretty good" superintendents can do leadership or management well. Excellent, futuristic superintendents do both in a focused, targeted, aligned, and highly communicative manner. We want to be both good leaders and good managers.

The Ultimate Application

The following questions are designed to assist you in applying higher-level thinking skills through application. Either alone or in a group setting, respond to each question based upon your own knowledge, experience, and further research.

1. Develop a model to be used by the school district in determining how to identify and prioritize system-wide needs that will be used in creating the vision, goals, budget, and staff development.

2. Identify and analyze factors that contribute to low and high faculty, staff, and other administrator morale.

3. Describe the relationship between faculty morale and organizational efficiency and productivity.

4. Evaluate and make recommendations concerning procedures and policies used in your district for the legal and equitable selection of new employees. What suggestions could you make for improving the process?

5. Describe the learning environment within your district. Explain your role within both the district and community in facilitating a safe, efficient, and effective learning environment.

6. Describe a plan whereby districts work with other stakeholders to enhance the organizational oversight of the district.

7. Create a budget development process that utilizes the knowledge and gifts of the learning community and is aligned with the district vision and goals.

Creating a Collaborative Learning Community

"As for being President, I feel like the man who was tarred and feathered and ridden out of town on a rail. To the man who asked him how he liked it, he said, 'If it wasn't for the honor of the thing, I'd rather walk.'"

—Abraham Lincoln

Standard 4: A school district leader who has the knowledge and ability to promote the success of all students by collaborating with families and other community members, responding to diverse community interests and needs, and mobilizing community resources

INTRODUCTION

One of the most interesting major cities of antiquity was Babylon. The ruins of Babylon are located in a dry and arid region about 600 miles east of the Suez Canal north of the Persian Gulf. The city had no natural resources upon which to develop the wealth and beauty for which it is known. There were no trees and little stone with which to build buildings, and its location was not on a major trade route. Everything was made out of sheer grit and determination.

What Babylon did have was fertile soil and water from the nearby Euphrates River. Yet the Babylonians had no way to get water from the Euphrates to the city. Thus, they developed one of the greatest and earliest engineering marvels by building canals that brought water from the river to the city. With this water, they were able to utilize their fertile soil to grow the crops they needed both for themselves and, eventually, others via the trade routes that would eventually develop.

Because writing paper as we know it today had not yet been invented, the Babylonian people wrote painstakingly on moist clay tablets, which were left to bake in the sun. They recorded everything, from daily events to business records. Vast libraries of these clay tablets have been found and deciphered through the years. The only known description of Babylon during its prime was recorded by someone from outside the kingdom, the Greek traveler and historian Herodotus. Herodotus wrote of the fertile soil, abundant crops, customs of the people, and the appearance of the city itself.

The rulers of Babylon were not known for plundering other peoples. Instead, the opposite was often true: other rulers attacked Babylon to try to get to the vast riches inside the city. However, this never worked. In all of its long history, Babylon was never captured by any enemy. Instead, Babylon is remembered for rulers with "wisdom, enterprise and justice" (Clason, 1955, p. 158).

One of the main reasons that invading tribes could not conquer Babylon was the huge walls surrounding the city, which were built and reinforced over many years. The walls were begun under the direction of Queen Semiramis during the early years of the city. The remains of these early walls have not been located, although the ruins of the larger and more famous walls have been found. These impenetrable walls were started about 600 BCE by King Nabopolassar and completed under the reign of his son, Nebuchadnezzar. The fall of Babylon did not occur due to the walls being overtaken. Instead, Babylon began its descent due to poor planning and decision making by King Nabonidus.

Nabonidus lost his confidence, took his eyes off the vision of Babylon, and became afraid. He feared that the invading army of Cyrus was going to get through the walls. To try to avoid defeat, he agreed to go outside the walls to fight with Cyrus himself. History shows this to be a bad decision, as Nabonidus lost without anyone having to assail the city walls. Once Cyrus defeated Nabonidus, the Babylonian walls were opened, and the invading army marched without resistance into Babylon. Although the city of Babylon now lies in ruins, which archeologists love to explore, the wisdom and grandeur of its original beauty and wealth live on in history and legend.

The example of Babylon is a good one for superintendents to keep in mind as they seek to collaborate with families and other community members, respond to diverse community interests and needs, and mobilize community resources for a common purpose. Superintendents, like the early Babylonians, must try to be proactive in relating to the needs of the community, whether by designing and building great canals to bring the Euphrates water to their arid city or by creating innovative ways to achieve the impossible in today's changing society.

Superintendents, like the early rulers of Babylon, do not see opposing groups as enemies to be attacked; rather, they build the necessary protections to ensure the district will be protected fiscally, legally, and ethically so all students can have the opportunity to learn. Superintendents do not view the success of the district, as identified as student learning within classrooms, as a competition but as a "together we win" outcome. Above all, each superintendent seeks to be known and remembered as someone with the "wisdom, enterprise and justice, and common sense"(Clason, 1955, p. 158) to do what is pragmatic, ethical, and necessary in creating a diverse yet collaborative learning community that works to improve life for everyone.

Thus, as shown in Figure 5.1, standards-based superintendents collaborate with families and other community members, respond to community interests and needs, and mobilize community resources.

Figure 5.1   Standards-Based Superintendents Are Collaborative

- Collaborate with families and other community members.
- Respond to community interests and needs.
- Mobilize community resources.

Source: Quincey & Kimberley Miller

PHILOSOPHICAL FRAMEWORK

Collaborating With Families and Other Community Members

We have all heard it said that no man is an island, meaning we cannot achieve everything we want or need alone. The same thing can be said for school districts and the communities they serve. The basic functions of a democratic society also cannot be created alone. We need each other. Recent data continues to show that districts and campuses that work closely with their constituents have consistently shown greater productivity than those who do not (Christopher, 2007; Dillon & Vail, 2005; Pascopella, 2004; Wasserman, 2004). Therefore, districts that demonstrate the ability to facilitate the planning and implementation of programs and services that bring together the various and diverse talents and resources of families and the community positively impact student learning. This can be done through multiple means, such as using public information and research-based knowledge of various current issues and trends to collaborate with community members and organizations. Applying a good understanding of community relations models as well as marketing strategies and processes and data-driven decision making and communication theories to craft frameworks for schools, businesses, community, government, and higher education partnerships are also important. An excellent example of school districts working in collaboration with a university will be shown in Chapter 8, where the development and implementation of a doctoral program in educational leadership utilizing the servant-leadership model is described (Greenleaf, 1982, 1991).

Again, using the "no man is an island" analogy, the days when school districts "did their own thing" in isolation from their surrounding communities have gone the way of rabbit ears on television sets. Although some may still use rabbit ears, their pictures are likely not as good as they would be with cable, high-definition, plasma, Blu-ray, or satellite connectivity. The same is true for districts that seek to operate in isolation or in ways that worked only in the past. They simply will not be as good as they could be if they sought to involve the community in goal setting and combined, aligned collaboration, decision making, and resource management. That is why superintendents who seek to optimize their effectiveness will have the desire and ability to develop and implement plans for nurturing relationships with community leaders. They will also reach out to different business, religious, political, and service organizations to strengthen programs and to support district goals.

These things can be done through involving community members, groups, and other stakeholders in district decision making and by reflecting an understanding of strategies to capitalize on the district's integral role in the larger community. Superintendents can show these skills by collaborating with community agencies that integrate health, social, and other services within the district to address student and family conditions that affect learning. Most of us know and understand that there are many, many "noneducational" things that impact student learning, such as drugs, alcohol, lack of money to pay the bills, divorce, absentee parents, homelessness, pregnancies, bullying, and multiple other issues that produce fear and conflict. Students do not, and cannot, forget their home environments when they walk through the doors of the school. They bring who they are and their individual circumstances with them. That is why it is so critically important that we work with as many groups as possible to provide for the needs, and often the healing, that so many students and families need.

In addition to all this, none of us can forget the ever-present media. In the days of printing presses, superintendents were warned to never pick a fight with anyone who "bought ink by the barrel." Although today's media may not buy ink by the barrel, they can be our friends, or they can, too often, be our worst enemies. Why is it that when great things happen in the schools, that is not news? But let something bad or questionable happen, it is on the front page, on the nightly news, and the talk of the supermarket. We know that we must do our best to develop, nurture, and sustain good media relations. We must develop community relationships that reflect our knowledge of effective media relations and model them effectively. Virtually all districts have their own policies and procedures for dealing with the media. Regardless of what those are, we must seek to work with the media to create a strong partnership to communicate the district's vision as well as our goals for getting us from today's reality to becoming the ideal district of the future.

Last, as shown in Figure 5.2, it is always important to develop and implement strategies that support the involvement of families in the education of their children in ways that reinforce for the district staff a belief that families have the best interests of their children in mind. Regretfully, we know that not every student is blessed with a nurturing, supportive family to encourage them in the importance of their education. Those are the students on whom we must focus even more attention and affirmation, because they are the ones who have the least of this super-important support network. They need us! The more we can do to increase family involvement in the schools for them and everyone else, the better society will be for all of us and for the future.

Figure 5.2   Families Are Important in the Education of Their Children

Source: Photo taken by Elizabeth Hall

Responding to Community Interests and Needs

Lyndon Johnson used to say that he wanted to know exactly who his enemies were so he could keep them close by. There will, unfortunately, be some people who just plain do not like us in our role as superintendents. This may be for strictly personal reasons or because they simply do not understand what is going on within the school district. They seem to think that anything they do not understand must, obviously, be our fault. Therefore, the superintendent is crazy, and everyone that works for the district must also be crazy.

That is not exactly the attitude that we are hoping to create within a collaborative community learning environment. To achieve a positive environment, culture, and climate, superintendents must facilitate and engage in activities so as to collect and organize formal and informal information from multiple stakeholders, even those who think we are crazy, as input into decision making. Remember what Lyndon Johnson said and keep those who do not like you close at hand. Try to figure out what is motivating their distrust or anger—and solve it.

One of the things we hear over and over is that superintendents do not really know what is going on within the campuses and in the community. Whether this is true or not is beside the point. It is what some people think, and their perception is their reality. Therefore, we should be as actively involved and visible in the community and on campuses as reasonably possible. No superintendent, nor any administrator, can be at every district and community event. It simply is not possible to be everywhere everyone wants you to be (see Figure 5.3). Prioritize what you can, and cannot, attend, but to the best of your ability, be visible, interested, friendly, and involved with differing groups. Seek to interact effectively with as many individuals and groups as possible, including those with conflicting perspectives.

Be able to assess, research, and plan for diverse district and community conditions and dynamics and to capitalize on the diversity of the community to improve district performance and student achievement. Remember, we are here to facilitate the best curriculum and instruction possible for all the students. No one should be left out, even if that student is not easy to teach or claims to have no interest whatsoever in learning or that school is deathly boring. It is our job to be the voice for those who cannot speak for themselves. It is up to us to be an advocate for students with special, unusual, and truly exceptional needs. After all, someone needs to be their advocate, and often their families do not know how. Never, ever,

Figure 5.3   Visibility Is Great, but You Can't Be Everywhere

Source: Dayton & Jenni Barone

ever give up on any student regardless of that child's needs, circumstances, or attitudes. Be diligent, committed, and persistent!

Mobilizing Community Resources

Not every resource is something that can be bought or sold. Many valuable assets are the talents, gifts, and resolve of community members who want to help teachers teach and students learn. As great superintendents, we display an understanding of and ability to use this vast community capital, including youth services that enhance student achievement, to solve district problems and to accomplish district goals. One way to do this is to join forces with other community groups, including municipalities, to address and solve issues of mutual concern. Superintendents can, thus, show an understanding of ways to use public resources and funds appropriately and cost-effectively to encourage communities and groups to provide new resources to address emerging student needs and problems. By all of us working together instead of separately, we can each achieve more. In this instance, the "more" is improving the lives and learning of students and families in our communities (see Figure 5.4). Now, *that* is a noble goal. Even if we cannot improve everyone's situation, we can improve life for some. And for those, our efforts will be worth it.

Figure 5.4   Family Needs Are Our Needs

Source: Photo taken by Isabel Rendon-Peta

PROBLEM-BASED LEARNING

Collaborating With Families and Other Community Members: The Answer's Not Blowing in the Wind

When Quinnten McIntyre was hired by the board of San Augustine School District, they were impressed by his intelligence, experience, confidence, and steady, even-keeled manner. As a new superintendent, these attributes served him particularly well, because he followed a highly volatile superintendent who did not seem to get along well with virtually anyone. In the beginning, Quinnten's calm demeanor seemed like a refreshing change of pace.

However, as time went by, the very aspects of his personality that originally had attracted the board seemed to become the things that caused Quinnten difficulties. Because he was by nature a quiet, "get the job done from behind the scenes" leader, people inside and outside the district began to see him as a loner, aloof, and standoffish. Although Quinnten did join various civic clubs and organizations, he seemed consistently to stay on the sidelines. While always polite, he did not show signs of overt interest and friendliness or volunteer for anything in the community. In short, he did not go out of his way to create relationships with other civic and community members and organizations that could have resulted in mutually beneficial outcomes for everyone. Quinnten preferred to work as a "one-man band" rather than as a group collaborator and community consensus builder and leader.

Over time, these attributes did not serve him well. People felt they knew him on the outside but not on the inside. His initially perceived calm demeanor came to be seen as an indicator of having no drive or overt passion toward working with the district community to set goals of mutual benefit or determine how the school district fit into the bigger picture of enhancing the town. The entire concept of networking and collaborating seemed to elude his consciousness and understanding.

The board began to wonder quietly how these traits could have escaped them in the superintendent search process. Because the previous superintendent had been such an obvious extrovert, had they let the pendulum swing too far in the opposite direction by hiring someone who wasn't just calm but a downright ultra-introvert? As their phones began to ring with citizen concerns, they had to wonder if they had gone wrong and, if so, what now could be done to fix the situation.

Reflective Practice: Pause and Think

Through the use of reflection and higher-order thinking skills, address the following questions:

1. What safeguards could the board have put into place during the search process to prevent a situation like this from arising?

2. Develop and propose a set of questions that could be asked of superintendent candidates to delve into their skills as collaborators and facilitators and elicit more than placid, expected responses to get at who they really are and how they really lead.

3. How should the board proceed in working together with Quinnten to improve his school and community relationships?

4. After meeting with the board about their concerns, Quinnten is offended. He feels he is not being given a fair amount of time to implement his leadership style. While he does feel that being a part of the community is important, he does not see the value of using his limited time to develop and nurture relationships with anyone outside of district employees. He feels his efforts are best spent inside the office working to improve teaching and learning. How would you respond, and why? Support your answers.

5. After meeting with the board and discussing their concerns, Quinnten decides it may be in the best interest of his district longevity to change his ways. Generate a plan by which Quinnten can seek to develop the relationships he has not pursued in the past.

6. As Quinnten begins to try to mend fences in the school community, he meets with mixed results. Some people seem pleased to see him seek to become more involved. Others are skeptical. Still others appear to be keeping their distance from him with an attitude of "too little, too late." What should Quinnten's response be to those he approaches and, particularly, to those who question his apparent change of heart? Justify his response in a convincing manner.

Responding to Community Interests and Needs: The Faint of Heart Need Not Apply

The Aurora School District has a long and respected history. It was the first district in the state to offer free public kindergarten and 12th grade for all students. It was known for having the courage to pilot innovative and controversial educational methods, such as a nongraded curriculum and open classrooms in the 1960s and 1970s. With Aurora high schools having long been known for their innovation and the quality of their graduates both in the workforce and entering college, graduates considered their alma maters with pride. They had received a quality public education and knew it.

However, through the years, things slowly began to change in Aurora. After the Vietnam War, thousands of refugees were relocated in and around Aurora due to its proximity to the ocean. Students from these families brought a new and entirely different challenge to the educators of Aurora. At the same time, other cultural groups were also growing in numbers, while the district simultaneously began experiencing "white flight" to the suburbs.

Over the next three decades, the district was unsuccessful in keeping abreast with changing times and demographics. Board elections and meetings became contentious. Teachers and administrators were moved from campus to campus on a regular basis in an effort to achieve racial balance. The sense of unity and pride that had so encapsulated the district in the past seemed to be gone forever. Test scores were going down, morale was at an all-time low, beautiful older buildings were falling into disrepair, and teachers were leaving for jobs in other districts where people got along. Furthermore, industry tax dollars seemed to be drying up as business in the area suffered a downturn. How could things have changed so much?

The board of trustees is now looking for a new superintendent (again) to come in, turn things around, bring people with highly divergent views together, increase student learning, and restore the pride in Aurora schools. Yet people across the state are aware of the issues in the problem-ridden district. Many potentially good candidates have dire concerns about applying for the superintendency of such a topsy-turvy district. The unofficial slogan for the job posting became "The faint of heart need not apply."

Reflective Practice: Pause and Think

1. Hindsight is always 20/20. However, what are some things that could have been done to avoid letting the district "fall from glory" in such a fashion?

2. What can be learned from the Aurora experience to use in districts undergoing change that you may someday lead?

3. Synthesize the Aurora situation. What would be the attributes of a perfect candidate for this job? Why?

4. If you were an applicant for this position, what would make you the best person for improving everything from district moral to student performance? How would you improve your skills to enhance your capabilities?

5. Develop an implementation plan for the first 100 days of the new superintendent's being on the job. What exactly should the new leader seek to do in prioritized order, and why?

6. Perhaps one of the hardest things to be done in Aurora is to restore a sense of pride in both the schools and the community. The culture and climate of the school district is critically important to how the community sees itself as well as to how others see it. In what ways can the new superintendent utilize visibility, communication, and interaction skills with greatly divided peoples to improve and restore pride to this once-renowned school district?

Mobilizing Community Resources: Jimmy Cracked Corn, and We Do Care

The City of Ortievo and the Ortievo School District have enjoyed a collaborative relationship for many years. Recently, they have taken this relationship to a new level. Due to the joint efforts of a proactive superintendent and mayor, the two are now cosponsoring several venues that neither of them could have afforded alone; Yet by combining resources, jointly applying for targeted federal funds, and applying visionary leadership, the school district and city are providing the citizens of Ortievo with resources they would not have been able to afford without this collaboration.

One good example is the support of the school district for the construction and opening of an indoor-outdoor Olympic-sized swimming pool, which is owned by the city. Whereas the city had the funds to build the pool, it was concerned about ongoing operating costs. Admission fees would cover the costs for the summer, but both groups wanted to keep the pool open year-round on a limited basis by using a sliding roof to enclose it in the winter. Senior citizens and others supported this idea, because it would provide them an indoor pool in which to exercise in the winter months. But with school in session, no children would be using the pool during the day.

Through joint discussions in open session between the city council and school board, the district budgeted funds to help defray the winter operating costs of the pool. In exchange, the district swim teams could use the facilities as their practice and performance pool without paying additional fees. The district could also host various swim team events and competitions where other swim teams from out of town would also use the pool. This would increase tourism to the city, and more money would be spent on lodging, food, and entertainment.

Another example involves a city park with multiple basketball courts, tennis courts, and soccer fields but no electricity to allow for play after dark. Again, through the use of a mutually developed grant, funds were obtained whereby the city and schools now cosponsor several well-lit facilities on both city and school property. Other examples of the city and schools working together for mutual goals include the installation of bicycle lanes on public streets running close to schools and the mutual support of economic development issues for the greater good of the community.

Reflective Practice: Pause and Think

1. What are the pros and cons, including liability issues, of schools and cities working together on projects such as these?

2. Identify other examples of ways cities and schools can work together to meet mutual needs.

3. With what entities besides municipalities can schools work collaboratively to help students be successful? Provide examples of both what these would be and how they would be important.

4. One of the most specific needs inside school districts is enhancing student learning. In what ways can the district work with other community resources, such as youth and social services, to improve teaching and learning?

5. Describe and explain collaborative projects that you have seen that have worked to the mutual benefit of the different stakeholders. How could each be improved, or modified, if used again?

6. As a superintendent, brainstorm ideas to seek creative new ways to mobilize community resources appropriately and effectively to address student needs and problems. Be specific.

ASSESSMENT MODEL

Standard 4: A school district leader who has the knowledge and ability to promote the success of all students by collaborating with families and other community members, responding to diverse community interests and needs, and mobilizing community resources

In Table 5.1, you will find a planning rubric for assessing your progress toward this standard. Vertical and horizontal mentoring are important elements in maximizing your success. For additional reading on administrator induction and mentoring, see *Principal Induction: A Standards-Based Model for Administrator Development* (Wilmore, 2004).

Table 5.1 Planning Rubric for Standard 5

Element	Goals to Meet Standard for Improved School District Leadership	Specific Activities Designed to Achieve Standard	People and Resources Needed to Operationalize This Strategy	Date by Which Activity Will Be Completed	Evidence of Standard Attainment
4.1 Collaborate With Families and Other Community Members	a. Demonstrate the ability to facilitate the planning and implementation of programs and services that bring together the resources of families and the community to affect student learning positively.				
	b. Demonstrate an ability to use public information and research-based knowledge of issues and trends to collaborate with community members and community organizations to have a positive affect on student learning.				
	c. Apply an understanding of community relations models, marketing strategies and processes, data-driven decision making, and communication theory to craft frameworks for school, business, community, government, and higher education partnerships.				
	d. Demonstrate an ability to develop and implement a plan for nurturing relationships with community leaders and reaching out to different business, religious, political, and service organizations to strengthen programs and support district goals.				

	e. Demonstrate the ability to involve community members, groups, and other stakeholders in district decision making, reflecting an understanding of strategies to capitalize on the district's integral role in the larger community.			
	f. Demonstrate the ability to collaborate with community agencies to integrate health, social, and other services in the schools to address student and family conditions that affect learning.			
	g. Demonstrate the ability to conduct community relations that reflects knowledge of effective media relations and that models effective media relations practices.			
	h. Develop and implement strategies that support the involvement of families in the education of their children and reinforce for district staff a belief that families have the best interests of their children in mind.			
4.2 Respond to Community Interests and Needs	a. Facilitate and engage in activities that reflect an ability to inform district decision making by collecting and organizing formal and informal information from multiple stakeholders.			
	b. Demonstrate the ability to promote maximum involvement with and visibility within the community.			

(Continued)

83

Table 5.1 (Continued)

Element	Goals to Meet Standard for Improved School District Leadership	Specific Activities Designed to Achieve Standard	People and Resources Needed to Operationalize This Strategy	Date by Which Activity Will Be Completed	Evidence of Standard Attainment
	c. Demonstrate the ability to interact effectively with individuals and groups that reflect conflicting perspectives.				
	d. Demonstrate the ability to assess, research, and plan for diverse district and community conditions and dynamics and capitalize on the diversity of the community to improve district performance and student achievement.				
	e. Demonstrate the ability to advocate for students with special and exceptional needs.				
4.3 Mobilize Community Resources	a. Demonstrate an understanding of and ability to use community resources, including youth services that enhance student achievement, to solve district problems and accomplish district goals.				
	b. Demonstrate how to use district resources in conjunction with the community to solve issues of joint concern.				
	c. Demonstrate an understanding of ways to use public resources and funds to encourage communities to provide new resources to address emerging student problems.				

Ways for You to Do It:

A superintendent leader can enhance systematic school improvement by using the following strategies:

- Being proactive in developing business and other school community partnerships
- Being actively involved in the community, creating positive public relations, and being visible at campuses and other district entities
- Participate in ongoing research and brainstorming of new ways to improve efficiency, maximize finances and other resources, and foster divergent thinking within the school community and beyond
- Hosting regular informal community and district input meetings
- Hiring excellent employees; providing proper orientation, training, and mentoring; then giving them the freedom to do their jobs with appropriate support
- Minimizing the amount of time principals and other educators are required to attend off-campus meetings, etc., taking them away from student learning
- Encouraging, providing funding for, and supporting parent education and mentoring courses on issues that are timely and relevant to parents' unique situations.
- Soliciting teachers' and other educators' input on organizational and resource issues as much as practical
- Working to engage partnerships with local community colleges and universities to offer dual-credit courses at their or your own campuses for high school students and graduate courses for district employees to improve their knowledge, skills, and dispositions for student benefit
- Attending portions of as many teacher and other meetings as possible for visibility, to show support, and to learn something yourself as well as encouraging your staff to do likewise
- Knowing your district well, including being aware of the differing needs, populations, and campus situations inside and outside of classrooms
- Establishing student work programs with local businesses and industries to meet their varying needs
- Considering all viewpoints with an open mind and without hostility in dealing with conflict resolution
- Utilizing different types of teachers and other educators on various district and community committees
- Recognizing and appreciating all educators, staff, and volunteers for doing a good job

CONCLUSIONS

Working with our communities and the groups within them is of vital importance to the success of students. It is critical that we reach out to all segments of the community, including those who do not support the district or its vision. We should actively seek to collaborate with and engage as many people as possible in the school community to help us meet as many student needs as possible. We can do this by being visible and actively involved in the community, soliciting input and support from diverse perspectives in decision making, and working to create partnerships with multiple entities. We can also solicit solid working relationships with the media proactively rather than reactively.

We must always remember that we are here to be of service to the interests and needs of the community rather than the other way around. The district cannot maximize its productivity alone. We need the community, and the community needs us. The relationship must be a collaborative partnership with a common goal of improving society through a free and appropriate education for every student regardless of individual circumstances. We must also be proactive in seeking new ways to mobilize new and existing funds to meet the emerging needs of students in today's changing society. We cannot continue to do things the way they have worked successfully in the past. We must constantly be looking, searching, researching, and working collaboratively with others to address changing needs in a positive and successful way. Last, we must always evaluate everything we do to see if there is any way we can do anything, regardless of how minor, so as to result in improved teaching and learning. That is what our role is all about: improving teaching and learning.

The Ultimate Application

The following questions are designed to assist you in applying higher-level thinking skills through application. Either alone or in a group setting, respond to each question based upon your own knowledge, experience, and further research.

1. Describe ideal implications for solid support and community partnerships with the school district.

2. Give examples of the role of the superintendent in developing collaborative partnerships with external groups and agencies within the district community.

3. What are the effects of community partnerships on student achievement? How could these relationships be both researched and improved?

4. Explain the benefits of a diversified district environment and its relationship to the school community.

5. Compare and contrast the pros and cons of having volunteers serving inside the school district. Include legal perspectives and draw conclusions.

6. Create a model to improve a school district's image in the community.

7. Discuss ways to encourage parents and others to become actively engaged in the schools. Include specific strategies for non-English-speaking persons and those from low-income areas.

8. Describe steps districts can take to generate community support in rural, suburban, and urban settings. Do the steps vary according to context? If so, explain them.

The Ethical District Leader

Standard 5: A school district leader who has the knowledge and ability to promote the success of all students by acting with integrity, fairness, and in an ethical manner

INTRODUCTION

There is an old story about a farmer, a fern, and a piece of bamboo. The farmer planted seeds for both a fern and a bamboo plant. He took good care of both of them. He made sure they got plenty of water and light. Soon, the fern sprang up; the bamboo did not. Time went by, and the fern continued to grow; the bamboo did not. The farmer continued to take care of both of them. A long time went by. The fern had become a beautiful, lush plant; the bamboo remained invisible.

But the farmer did not give up on the bamboo. A very long time went by, and he persisted in taking extra good care of both the fern plant and the bare patch of ground. People, of course, thought he was crazy. Why was he taking such good care of a bamboo seed planted long ago that had yielded absolutely nothing?

Yet the farmer continued on, even though no one else believed in his bamboo. Finally one day, he saw a tiny, tiny sprout appear from the bamboo seed. He joyfully continued to nurture and sustain it. In time, it continued to grow and grow and grow until the bamboo was six feet tall!

His family and friends were amazed! They asked the farmer why he had remained so committed to the bamboo when absolutely nothing was happening. He said that it takes some plants longer for their roots to develop and take hold than others. He explained that you cannot expect every living thing to grow or be exactly alike. You must have patience and remain faithful to the purpose you set out to achieve.

Cannot the same be said for good superintendents? Sometimes we have students, faculty, and even other administrators who blossom right away. But sometimes we have others who are like the bamboo. They need extra persistence, extra faithfulness, and extra commitment. Superintendents who display these qualities are displaying solid character attributes and will conduct themselves with fairness, integrity, and in a truly ethical manner. This is shown in Figure 6.1.

Figure 6.1 Standards-Based Superintendents Have a Moral Compass

- Act with integrity.
- Act fairly.
- Act ethically.

Source: Katie Harris

PHILOSOPHICAL FRAMEWORK

Acts With Integrity

Having integrity is a core value in most societies. We like to think we have and display it. Yet often we see things happening that display a lack of integrity. Do we sometimes demonstrate a similar lack of honor ourselves while simultaneously thinking we are the most honest people around?

For district and community members to trust us, we superintendents must display respect for the rights of others with regard to confidentiality and dignity. At the same time, all of our interactions should be honest and aboveboard. These attributes would likely be included in virtually anyone's list of important leadership characteristics. Yet in real life, they are often easier said than done. With things happening quickly all around us, complex decisions must be made in a timely manner. Often, it is difficult to please everyone. Thus, some may think you are not respecting their rights and opinions. Good superintendents have either an inborn or a developed skill to create a balance in addressing each situation individually and with integrity. They also ensure that each person involved is treated with dignity, concern, and in a manner that shows they, their thoughts, and their individual needs are cared about. Everything is not going to always go the way any single person or group, including yourself, wants. The difficult part comes in creating this balance through intrinsic and desired reflection that leads to moral leadership (Fullan, 2003; Pellicer, 2003).

Acts Fairly

This same rationale continues in treating persons, issues, things, programs, etc. in a fair manner. It is easy to have a perception of what something is and act on that perception without really knowing all the facts. Although none of us would like to admit it, upon close introspection, we could likely find at least one instance where we have felt strongly about something and did not want our perceptions being messed up with the facts (the truth). This is an easy pitfall to trip into. It can, and does, happen to nearly everyone. However, if it happens very often, other people's perception of us, as well as our leadership skills, can become negative. When others think we are being unfair to them, their program, their issue, or anything else, it is very hard to turn things around without a lot of open and direct communication and apologies. If it happens repeatedly, others will begin to perceive us as biased. They may even be right. Sometimes we do display bias even without knowing we are doing it.

That is why it is so critically important for superintendents to demonstrate the ability to combine impartiality, sensitivity to student diversity, and ethical considerations in interactions with others. In April 2007, "shock jock" Imus was fired from his radio and television positions for on-air insults of the Rutgers womens basketball team. Whether he meant them or not is not the issue here, nor are his profuse apologies. What matters is that he hurt young women he had never met with moral and racial slurs. No one appreciated it, and no one thought it was funny. Regardless of how many times he apologized, the harm was done. Imus did not consider how his words would hurt others. His moment of "fun" cost him his job and career (Kelley, Starr, & Conant, 2007).

In short, superintendents serve to fulfill the needs of all of the students, faculty, and community, not just the people who are ideal, show up every day, and never create problems. The superintendent is an activist for all students and the entire district learning community. The superintendent speaks up and takes a stand for the importance of a free and appropriate education for everyone and is sensitive to the diverse needs of all students, their families, and their interests and desires. It is the superintendent, in the end, who must model fair behavior that focuses on ethical considerations for all members of the district and learning community.

Acts Ethically

The model superintendent demonstrates and explains to others how they use their ethics in all decision making (Strike, 2007). The school community needs to know and understand why and how decisions are made. Often, people will have their own perceptions about what should have been done and will think you should have done exactly that. Until they know why you did what you did, they will continue to be unhappy. If this pattern of behavior doesn't change, their negativity will fester and become a problem in the community—and for you. That's why open decision making where all the facts and issues involved are explained is so critically important. Howard Gardner (Fryer & Gardner, 2007) says, "It's not enough to espouse high standards. To live up to them—and help others do the same—requires an ethical cast of mind that lets you practice your principles consistently (p. 51)."

Decisions must also be based upon legal and moral precepts. Something may make all the sense in the world, but if it isn't legal, obviously, it cannot be done. Often, citizens are unaware of every facet of different laws and regulations facing school districts today. This is particularly true in regard to issues such as public school finance and proposed construction bond elections. Therefore, citizens may have an idea for the solution to a problem and yet have no idea that it simply cannot be done because it is not legal. They still won't know unless we explain it to them. In fact, legal parameters should be explained early in any decision-making process to avoid anyone becoming invested and empowered in a solution that is simply not legal. All decisions must be both ethical and legal.

All of this may sound obvious, but acting with integrity, fairness, and in an ethical manner at all times is one of the most important functions of a superintendent. It is our role to be advocates for all the children in the district. We must model and promote the highest standards of conduct, ethical principles, and integrity in decision making, actions, and behaviors. To do any of these things, we must also know and apply knowledge of ethical issues that affect education (Wilmore, 2002). As superintendents, we must be abreast of current events that could impact our district and students. In today's rapidly changing and complex society, this means we must be aware of virtually everything.

PROBLEM-BASED LEARNING

Acts With Integrity: Please Don't Slay the Messenger

As superintendent of the Heaven on Earth School District, Bates Nelson suspects that one of his campus principals is misrepresenting him to the faculty. Bates gets along well with the principal and actually thinks highly of him, but he keeps getting reports of things he has supposedly said that the principal either distorted or outright lied about. This situation is beginning to cause Bates problems. He knows he should directly discuss the situation with the principal but hates to upset him in case the reports are untrue.

In an effort not to distress the principal needlessly, Bates sends for another campus administrator from the same school, Amelia LeGrand, in whom he has complete trust. He asks Amelia if the things he has heard are true. She shows discomfort for being put in what she perceives to be an awkward situation. Amelia hesitates to discuss the situation for fear it will come back to hurt her as well as the campus itself. Upon assurances from Bates that what she reveals will not go any farther and will be kept in complete confidence, Amelia tells Bates only what she has personally seen or heard.

Bates is not pleased. Soon after Amelia leaves his office, he contacts the principal in question for a meeting where he directly confronts him. Needless to say, the principal denies everything and demands to know where Bates heard such a story. Bates tells him that he has heard these reports from various people and, at first, found them hard to believe. However, he admits, he finally spoke with someone he trusts and found the stories to be true.

The principal immediately figures out who the "person he trusts" is and, sure enough, lets Amelia have it. From that point on, the principal makes campus life as difficult as possible for Amelia, which causes her great chagrin. She feels betrayed, even though she realizes Bates did not actually reveal her name. Still, her faith in Bates is ruined. Bates does not seem to understand why Amelia has cooled in her attitude toward him. From his perspective, he did nothing to harm her trust.

Reflective Practice: Pause and Think

Through the use of reflection and higher-order thinking skills, respond to the following questions:

1. Were Bates's actions toward the principal ethical? Toward Amelia? Explain your answer.

2. Were the campus principal's actions toward both Bates and Amelia ethical? Differentiate your responses.

3. As superintendent, what would you have done if faced with a similar scenario? Support your response.

4. Amelia ended up in a very awkward situation. If you were her, how would you have responded to Bates's request for information? How would you have responded to the principal when he treated you badly? Why?

5. How should Bates have originally responded to the reports about the principal?

6. After everything falls apart with both the principal and Amelia, is Bates's credibility destroyed forever? If not, how can Bates improve the situation?

Acts Fairly: Why Is This Happening to Me? What Did I Do Wrong?

Casey Westbrook has been very successful serving as principal of a highly diverse urban middle school known for being "rough." Not only have test scores improved but so have campus and community morale. Some long-standing problems have disappeared, and others have greatly improved. Casey is happy in his role and enjoys working with students and families from the neighborhood his school serves.

Based on Casey's success with this population, he was the natural choice to lead a new district-level program designed to improve collaborative relationships between the district and the community. The purpose of this collaborative was to improve student performance in high-risk populations. Although Casey was originally reluctant to leave his campus, the goals of this new program appealed to him greatly. He accepted the new position and went at it with passion and determination.

During his first year, the program's success succeeded initial expectations. Virtually everyone was pleased with his work and the impact it was having on student learning. Therefore, it came as a complete shock to Casey when his superintendent, Mr. Faust, asked him to give up his new position and return to being principal of his original school. Mr. Faust based this determination on the district's inability to find anyone to replace Casey and do nearly as good a job as principal at his original campus. The neighborhood and students were too difficult for just anyone to handle, Casey was told. Because he was so good at it, and because he had the new program off the ground and doing so well, Mr. Faust thought the best decision for the district was to move Casey back to his old position.

While Casey's head understood the rationale, his heart did not. He strongly felt he was being penalized for doing too good a job in both arenas. He tried to assure Mr. Faust that his new role was equally, if not more, demanding than his principalship. But he had done such a good job getting the new program going that he had made it look easy. In Mr. Faust's eyes, anyone could do the second role, but only Casey could handle the complexities of being principal of this particular school. Casey was devastated, but he did what he was asked to do. As time went by, it hurt him even more to see the new program he had worked so hard to develop and implement seem to fall apart in front of his very eyes. "How can Mr. Faust not see what is taking place?" his logic wondered. "And why was I punished for doing a good job?" cried out his heart.

Reflective Practice: Pause and Think

1. Although Casey did not question Mr. Faust's authority to move him, he did question his ethics. Was it fair of Mr. Faust to do this? Was his decision ethical?

2. Was Mr. Faust's decision based on sound reasoning?

3. Was Casey actually being "punished" for doing a good job?

4. Was it fair of Mr. Faust to ask Casey to return to his previous role even though he had asked him to perform the new one? Why, or why not?

5. Is Casey being overly sensitive? How would you react if the same thing happened to you? What would you do?

6. How can this awkward situation be turned into a win-win situation?

Acts Ethically: Is Equal Always Ethical? Or Is Ethical Always Equal?

As the new superintendent of Jefferson Schools, Odiella Hawthorne is taking her time studying and evaluating various district programs. Her goal is to make sure each program is fulfilling its objectives and is cost-effective and that all the diverse needs of students in the district population are being appropriately served.

As time goes by, Odiella proposes several changes to the board that she feels will improve district efficiency. One of the changes would move some programs from one director to another. As she has studied the organizational structure, she has learned that some programs should be combined or eliminated while she would like to initiate other needed programs. She feels that a realignment of programs and directors is needed to ensure a balance of responsibilities and efficiency for everyone. The board supports her realignment plan and votes to allow her to move forward with it.

Although the realignment will cause no job loss, almost all the program directors will receive one or more new programs while also losing some. In other words, their combination of roles will change. Even though this change was approved by the board of trustees, some administrators are not happy. They do not see the need for change and feel that being asked to take on new roles and give up others is unfair.

Reflective Practice: Pause and Think

1. Define and explain the role of organizational change, including the positives and negatives that people may experience.

2. Why is change necessary in this situation?

3. What did Odiella do right in examining the change process?

4. In what ways could Odiella have improved the articulation and implementation of her suggested changes?

5. How should Odiella address the concerns of the unhappy administrators?

6. After Odiella has implemented the plan, if the administrators remain disgruntled, what should she then do?

ASSESSMENT MODEL

> **Standard 5:** A school district leader who has the knowledge and ability to promote the success of all students by acting with integrity, fairly, and in an ethical manner

In Table 6.1, you will find a planning rubric for assessing your progress toward this standard. Vertical and horizontal mentoring are important elements in maximizing your success. For additional reading on administrator induction and mentoring, see *Principal Induction: A Standards-Based Model for Administrator Development* (Wilmore, 2004).

Table 6.1   Planning Rubric for Standard 5

Element	Goals to Meet Standard for Improved District Leadership	Specific Activities Designed to Achieve Standard	People and Resources Needed to Operationalize This Strategy	Date by Which Activity Will Be Completed	Evidence of Standard Attainment
5.1 Acts with Integrity	a. Demonstrate a respect for the rights of others with regard to confidentiality and dignity and engage in honest interactions.				
5.2 Acts Fairly	a. Demonstrate the ability to combine impartiality, sensitivity to student diversity, and ethical considerations in their interactions with others.				
5.3 Acts Ethically	a. Make and explain decisions based upon ethical and legal principles.				

Ways for You to Do It:

A superintendent leader can enhance systematic school improvement by using the following strategies:

- Being honest, fair, and legal even under controversial and stressful circumstances
- Being seen and involved in the schools as well as at district and community events—living in the public eye
- Respecting educators and all people as individuals as well as exercising caution about both conscious and subconscious favoritism.
- Being a servant leader and not esteeming your role over that of anyone else
- Being a positive and consistent role model
- Acting in an ethical manner, because actions always speak louder than words
- Never making exceptions to rules and policies for yourself or any family members
- Avoiding anything that might look like a conflict of interest, even if it is not
- Encouraging all employees to learn more about and appreciate other cultures and walks of life, again leading by example
- Emphasizing professionalism and high standards for all district employees and especially yourself, the "first face" of the district to the public and, therefore, responsible for setting the first standard
- Performing background checks on all employees, including other administrators, prior to hiring
- As much as is legally possible, handling disciplinary and ethical issues regarding others in private
- Never using district funds for personal use
- Utilizing district policies whereby parents, teachers, and others follow the appropriate chain of command before meeting with you
- Not tolerating racism, sexism, or any other form of discrimination
- Not blaming or put extra work on everyone for the errors of a few
- Being strong
- Standing by your convictions
- Remembering that you are human and, therefore, will sometimes make mistakes—admitting them, fixing them, and moving on

CONCLUSIONS

A case can be made that the superintendency is one of the hardest public occupations in America today due to the vast responsibility to make ethical and fair decisions. Each decision a superintendent makes and every encounter with a citizen, student, faculty member, or any other stakeholder creates either a positive or a negative impression. Therefore, it is of foremost importance that all superintendents constantly be vigilant to respect the rights of others as well as their confidentiality and dignity. It is essential to engage in honest interactions, to be impartial on all issues, to be sensitive to student and community diversity, and to make all decisions based on moral, ethical, and legal principles. We must be conscientious in each of these aspects of integrity. One bad decision can impact an entire school district and the community beyond. One offensive statement can hurt many people. It can also cost you your job. Ask Imus.

The Ultimate Application

The following questions are designed to assist you in applying higher-level thinking skills through application. Either alone or in a group setting, respond to each question based upon your own knowledge, experience, and further research.

1. Explain the particular need for superintendents, as well as all educators, to display the highest standard of integrity, fairness, and ethics. How and why should the superintendent be held to a different standard than anyone else?

2. Reflect on an instance where you felt an administrator acted in an unethical manner. How could the situation have been handled in a more responsible way?

3. Describe a situation in which a teacher or staff member acted in an unethical manner and you were, or could have been, brought in to address the instance. What did, or would, you have done?

4. A teachers' group is spreading information regarding a district issue that is inaccurate and potentially damaging. Although several lower-level administrators have discussed the issue with the group, these discussions have not solved the problem. How would you, as superintendent, handle the situation in an ethical as well as legal manner?

5. Prepare a set of guidelines that would be fair and ethical for the election of students for auditioned and/or elected positions, such as cheerleading and drill teams, where they would be representing the school district.

6. Describe a potentially volatile situation in which an employee has filed a grievance that needs an ethical and fair resolution before it escalates to the board level. How would you handle the situation? Why? Support your response.

District and School Community Politics

"Conflict is the irritant that creates the pearl."

—Anonymous

> ***Standard 6:*** A school district leader who has the knowledge and ability to promote the success of all students by understanding, responding to, and influencing the larger political, social, economic, legal, and cultural context

INTRODUCTION

We have two Pug dogs and a cat. Our cat, Yum, is 20 years old. She is set in her ways. She does not want to be messed with, nor does she want anyone sniffing of her tail. She likes things nice and quiet. And when she meows, she wants you to come take care of her needs right this minute. Please believe that in her full 20 years of life, she has learned to be incredibly persistent. She has us well trained. We have become her staff.

Lacie is our 3-year-old fawn-colored Pug. She loves people almost as much as she loves to eat. She will eat anything, including clementines. She used to eat limes, too, but she gave them up. Lacie is warm, very loving, and a little bit bashful around other dogs other than our 1-year-old little black Pug, Annabella Rose. We call her Rose. Rose's disposition is totally different from Lacie's. She eats, but food does not drive her existence as it does Lacie's. She loves people like Lacie does, but do not expect Rose to give you kisses. It is not happening. Lacie will kiss you indefinitely. However, when other dogs come to play, Lacie will likely sniff her "Hello!" then go hide in her bed, whereas Rose will mix it up and play till they all drop from exhaustion. She does not have a bashful bone in her cute little black body.

Lacie the Pug and Yum the Cat have decided to mutually live and let live. They peacefully coexist by leaving each other alone. Rose has not learned that lesson. She never quits trying to play with Yum, who does *not* want to participate in such foolishness. Rose is fascinated with Yum's tail because it is straight. As a Pug, her own tail curls on top of her back. She cannot figure out Yum's tail and really, really, really wants to sniff it and, hopefully, paw it, every chance she gets. This, of course, sends Yum into a meowing frenzy, at which point we appear to rescue her from Rose. As I said, we are Yum's staff.

Are pets really so different from people? Some get along. Some do not. Some are friendly and loving. Others are not. Some are fascinated with those who are different. Others are not. Some want to be left alone. Some want to interact with everyone. Some choose not to participate in anything extra. Others take to their beds.

Superintendents have to deal with all of these diverse people. Often, it is not easy. Yet an area of the job that cannot be overemphasized is how superintendents must learn to understand, respond to, and influence the larger political, social, economic, legal, and cultural contexts of the district.

PHILOSOPHICAL FRAMEWORK

Understanding the Larger Context

It is important to see the global picture in regard to everything that can, or could, impact education and your district (Hoyle et al., 2005). This includes a wide variety of issues, including politics, society, economics, legalities, and cultural contexts (see Figure 7.1). It is easy to get so caught up in the day-to-day operations of the district that you lose sight of the larger political and societal issues that impact education daily (Leithwood, 1995). Seeing this big picture is what Standard 6 is all about.

Figure 7.1   Superintendents Seem to Be Everything to Everyone

Standards-Based Superintendents Serve as Politicians, Sociologists, Economists, Legal Experts, and Contemporary Cultural Anthropologists

- Understand the larger context.
- Respond to the larger context.
- Influence the larger context.

Source: Dayton & Jenni Barone

To do this appropriately, superintendents must have a good working knowledge and be able to apply that knowledge to research methods, theories, and concepts as they pertain to the operation of the district. As discussed in Chapter 6, decisions must be made from facts, not perceptions or preconceived notions. We cannot know the facts or be able to analyze and apply them properly without first being able to apply sound research methods and theories to district operations.

For example, superintendents need to have a sound understanding of poverty and its complex causes as well as other disadvantages that affect students, families, the school district, and the community. Understanding the work of Ruby Payne (2005, 2006) and others on language acquisition needs and strategies for children in poverty can be highly beneficial. Students from low-socioeconomic areas often learn in different ways and can be more tactile-kinetic than others. This can translate into difficulty focusing and sitting still for extended periods in the classroom. Educators who continue to try to teach students in traditional environments are, thus, less likely to achieve maximum learning effectiveness than those who adapt their teaching styles to meet their students' nontraditional learning styles. Every attempt should be made to provide teachers with the necessary teaching strategies to meet the diverse needs of all students, even when learning new techniques and changing established habits results in some initial uneasiness from moving out of their comfort zones.

Federal and state laws and regulations change rapidly, so a superintendent's learning curve never flattens out as the leader strives to keep up with them and how they impact the district. As shown in Figure 7.2, the superintendent deals with a continuous cycle of new legislation, designing ways of implementing the new legislation, and having even more new rules and regulations come on top of that. In this area, a superintendent must be in tip-top readiness at all times, because rarely does anything impact a district as much as legislation and regulation. A classic example of this is the federal No Child Left Behind Act (NCLB) with its myriad objectives and consequences. Conflicting opinions and regulations on how it should be implemented, variances and confusion between states on its implementation, and a lack of promised funding to help achieve its goals confuse both its implementation and evaluation. However, on a more positive side, NCLB has put an additional focus on increased achievement for all students, lessening the achievement gaps among ethnic, gender, and poverty subgroups and, definitely, increasing accountability by states and districts.

Figure 7.2   Let the Legislative Fun Begin

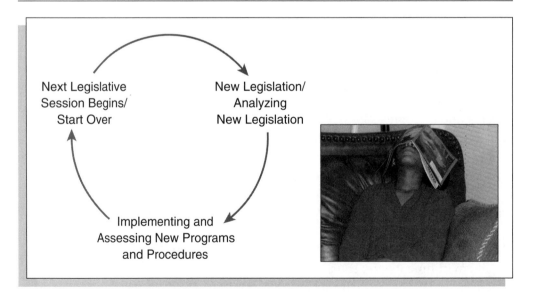

Source: Quincey & Kimberley Miller

Another significant issue facing superintendents is to understand and be able to explain to others the various ways in which public schools are funded. Although federal regulations and funding are similar from state to state, each state has its own formula for how state funds are distributed to individual school districts. In Texas, for example, the financing of the public schools has been in and out of court for years. Each time, the court has instructed the legislature to solve the problems of inequity. Every two years, and sometimes in special sessions, the Texas legislature meets and puts Band-Aids on the school finance problems, which eventually end up landing them back in court again. It is a cycle that does not appear to be ending any time soon. Texas serves as just one example of many of funding public education in a free and democratic society.

Yet superintendents in Texas and elsewhere must stay on top of each of the changing school finance plans, even knowing they are likely to change again soon. Each set of rules and funding formulas has a tremendous impact on the state funds each district will receive. This, in turn, has a direct impact on the district budget and the adopted local tax rate. Often, tax rates and budgets cannot be adopted until the last minute, after waiting to see how much money individual districts will receive from their states. This makes it very difficult for superintendents and school boards to plan for everything, from meeting the bare necessities for teaching and learning to employee salaries to special programs (Townsen, 2007). Superintendents, as the chief operating officers of the school district, have a tremendous responsibility to advocate for the needs of all students in today's changing society. Unfortunately, this seldom proceeds smoothly, as there are always more needs than available funds. As priorities are researched and identified, conflicts can arise, reinforcing the importance of excellent communication skills to explain legalities as well as the decision-making process utilized to identify budgeting priorities across the district.

One way that superintendents serve in this advocacy position is through developing and enhancing relationships with political leaders at the local, state, and national level. Having an individual, as well as a collective, voice through professional associations, such as the American Association of School Administrators and its state affiliates, is very important. Politicians often rely on their staffers to research prioritized needs and demands. Superintendents, other educators, and the professional organizations work collectively and independently to ensure that politicians and their staffers are acutely aware of the needs of students in schools today, the problems districts face, and the research-based realities, rather than the rhetoric, of what is necessary to improve teaching and learning.

The result of this networking and, yes, lobbying, is new laws, regulations, and legislation that will have a direct impact on school districts.

Superintendents must understand the legislation such that they can clearly articulate a position as to how new or proposed policy changes would benefit or harm their districts. They likewise must to be able to explain how proposed policies and laws can improve educational and social opportunities within their local districts. As shown in Figure 7.3, the cycle continues as superintendents apply these new mandates in the districts they lead.

Figure 7.3   Legislative Impact

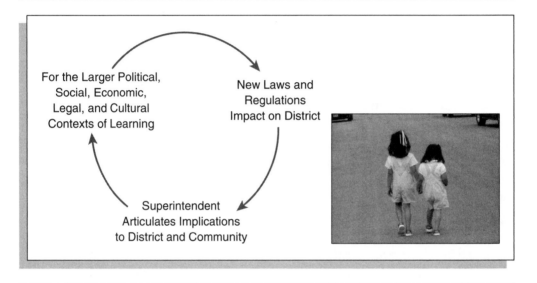

Source: Photo taken by Elizabeth Hall

Responding to the Larger Context

To go from "understanding" the larger context to "responding" is taking a step up Bloom's taxonomy into midlevel thinking skills. To respond, the superintendent must already understand the influences in play. In responding, the superintendent demonstrates the ability to engage students, parents, members of the school board, and other community members in advocating for adoption of improved policies and laws. In other words, the superintendent must not only understand these issues but go beyond to engage others in actively advocating for improved policies and laws that will benefit student learning.

To do this, superintendents must understand the larger political, social, economic, legal, and cultural contexts of laws and policies that impact the district. In addition, the superintendent also works collaboratively with others to research and develop activities and policies that will benefit their own students. They also must have the ability to communicate regularly with all segments of the district community, articulating trends, issues, and policies. Therefore, the superintendent's role as an advocate for students' needs transitions into a statesmanlike role of promoting the greater good of society through the education of our young.

Influencing the Larger Context

We started with *understanding* the larger political, social, economic, legal, and cultural contexts that impact school district leadership. Next, we moved up a step in Bloom's taxonomy to *responding* to the same issues and their potential impact. Now, we are going to the very top of the taxonomy by moving past understanding and responding to *influencing* others. At this level of performance, the superintendent develops lines of communication with local, state, and federal authorities and actively advocates for improved policies, laws, and regulations affecting public education, both directly as well as through organizations representing schools, educators, or others with similar interests. Consider this a marriage of excellent communication skills with networking and political skills for the purpose of creating improved laws and policies that benefit education for the greater good of society.

Consequently, superintendents advocate for policies and programs that promote equitable learning opportunities and success for all students, regardless of socioeconomic background, ethnicity, gender, disability, or other individual characteristics. The superintendent becomes the voice for every student and every issue that impacts their education. You become not only the manager of the fiscal and academic sides of the district but also an overt activist for moving forward, never resting, with a zeal and passion for improved teaching and learning. Superintendents do what is necessary and prudent to achieve those goals, even when such a role moves them out of their comfort zones.

PROBLEM-BASED LEARNING

Understanding the Larger Context: It's What's Inside That Counts, or Beauty Is Only Skin Deep

Gordon Lightfoot has been superintendent of The Academy at the Groves, a charter school that specializes in differentiated learning strategies for atypical learners, since it began five years ago. He is looked upon as the "face and voice" of the school. His passion and zeal have led the

Academy to its highest enrollment ever of 537 students. The school utilizes a former shopping center for its campus. During the last three years, many facilities improvements have taken place at The Academy, including adding needed classroom space and many campus beautification projects. In fact, there have recently been so many campus beautification projects that teachers and some parents are becoming concerned that Mr. Lightfoot's priorities have shifted from enhancing their differentiated learning strategies and techniques, for which the school is chartered and known, to a more superficial emphasis on how things look. In his defense, Mr. Lightfoot reminds them that as a charter school they are very dependent on student enrollment for their funding. He strongly feels that it is important for the campus to look appealing as an enticement to parents, students, visitors, and potential sources of external funding. Although few disagree that the original shopping center motif was not inviting to students, they still feel that so much money is being spent on how things look, the academics as well as the number, quality, salaries, and workload of faculty are at risk of deteriorating.

Mr. Lightfoot does not see their concerns as valid. Leading The Academy with a "strong arm," he puts more and more pressure on the teachers to go far beyond their original workloads with no help in sight. With morale sagging, teachers are becoming discouraged and disgruntled. Some have already left The Academy, and others are looking to leave. Still, Mr. Lightfoot appears to have absolutely no understanding whatsoever that there is a problem. As long as things look good on the outside, and things appear to be going well on the inside, he is convinced the school is in good shape. He is proud of how nice the campus now looks. The overwork of the teachers rarely, if ever, crosses his mind. When it does, he sees their concerns as merely whining, and with regard to those who leave, he sees their departures as a good riddance.

Reflective Practice: Pause and Think

Through the use of reflection and higher-order thinking skills, respond to the following questions:

1. Compare and contrast public financing of charter schools with that of traditional school districts in your state.

2. What characteristics of your state funding system could be applied to The Academy at the Groves?

3. What role, if any, would the board of a public charter school have in situations such as this?

4. What leadership theories would apply to this situation? Draw comparisons and make conclusions.

5. How can a common understanding be developed between the divergent perspectives of Superintendent Lightfoot and the teachers?

6. To what extent should the campus appearance determine budget priorities? Give examples.

Responding to the Larger Context: Change for the Sake of Change, or Too Much Change Too Fast?

Leonard Peterson follows Guy Simon as superintendent of Fidelity Springs School District upon Guy's retirement after 25 years of notable service. The district has experienced considerable growth and is now facing challenges associated with that growth. After his first three years at Fidelity Springs, Leonard becomes convinced it is time to begin an aggressive building campaign. He spends considerable amounts of his time and efforts trying to persuade others likewise.

Although most people agree that additional facilities are needed, most of his administrative team does not feel that as aggressive a building campaign as Leonard wants is absolutely necessary at this time. They would prefer to add a building at a time rather than several simultaneously. They believe that by adding one campus at a time, the district can better absorb the construction costs and not have to go as deeply into debt or put an unreasonable burden on taxpayers.

Leonard strongly disagrees and goes so far as to say that whoever is not "with him" on this project is "against" him. Most of the people against the more aggressive building project do not consider themselves as being against Leonard. They simply consider themselves as being more prudent with taxpayer dollars and do not see the urgency of building so many campuses at the same time. They would also like to investigate adding on to some of the current buildings rather than starting totally from scratch. Leonard does not want to add on to existing buildings, saying that core elements, such as the cafeterias and libraries, could not handle the extra student load.

Thus, Leonard and his administrative team have reached an impasse. Leonard wants to go to the board with a unified plan. Because he has made it plain that if his team members do not support his plan they are "against" him, they have become afraid for their jobs. The culture and climate within Fidelity Springs is suffering as an attitude of fear permeates the central administration building.

Reflective Practice: Pause and Think

1. Compare and contrast the distinctions between *understanding* and *responding to* change efforts.

2. In this instance, is Leonard or his leadership team being unreasonable? Either of them? Both of them? Explain your response.

3. What data, issues, and trends should Leonard and his leadership team be looking at in addition to increased student enrollment?

4. Because Leonard is the superintendent and the others work for him, is it important that he cares what they think? Why doesn't he go to the board without their approval? What impact would this action have, if any?

5. In what ways would the larger political, social, economic, legal, and cultural contexts of the district impact decision making regarding this proposed building campaign? In each instance, be specific.

6. What would you recommend as a solution to this stalemate?

Influencing the Larger Context: Let's Define *Justice*

Enrique Villarreal is superintendent of the Sabine-Neches School District, a small school district with low property values. His district has been adversely affected by various new state laws regarding school funding for areas in poverty. His concern is that the legislature is trying to force smaller districts to consolidate with other districts by default due to decreased funding. By lowering their state formula funding by small amounts each year, the legislature has made it increasingly difficult for this district to stay afloat, much less to be able to offer advanced courses and extracurricular activities. By slowly "starving them to death," Enrique feels the state legislature is forcing his district to join with others for survival.

Enrique and the citizens of his town are opposed to merging with another district. They feel that when a community loses its school district, it will eventually lose its identify. Through the years, Enrique has become more and more politically active by targeting his own representatives and other state legislators on behalf of small school funding. In fact, he has created such a reputation as a voice for small and low-property-value districts that he was recently elected president of the Justice Center, an entity that supports equity issues for all schools. As a group, school districts collectively address their needs with more clout than any of them would have had as an individual district. Enrique hopes that his involvement in the Justice Center will influence the larger context within which small school districts operate.

Reflective Practice: Pause and Think

1. What lines of communication are necessary to develop and implement to influence larger contexts beyond your immediate sphere of influence?

2. In what ways can such lines of communication be established, nurtured, and sustained?

3. Provide examples of advocacy groups, such as the Justice Center, of which you are aware or in which you are active that address specific issues. What are these issues? What is your involvement, if any?

4. In what other ways could Enrique and the citizens of Sabine-Neches influence the larger political context regarding small school districts?

5. In what ways could Enrique involve his board and the boards of other districts similar to his own in addressing funding and other issues?

6. Compare and contrast the benefits and drawbacks of very small school districts. Are they worth protecting? Defend and substantiate your response.

ASSESSMENT MODEL

> **Standard 6:** A school district leader who has the knowledge and ability to promote the success of all students by understanding, responding to, and influencing the larger political, social, economic, legal, and cultural context

In Table 7.1, you will find a planning rubric for assessing your progress toward this standard. Vertical and horizontal mentoring are important elements in maximizing your success. For additional reading on administrator induction and mentoring, see *Principal Induction: A Standards-Based Model for Administrator Development* (Wilmore, 2004).

Table 7.1 Planning Rubric for Standard 6

Element	Goals to Meet Standard for Improved School District Leadership	Specific Activities Designed to Achieve Standard	People and Resources Needed to Operationalize This Strategy	Date by Which Activity Will Be Completed	Evidence of Standard Attainment
6.1 Understand the Larger Context	a. Demonstrate the ability to use appropriate research methods, theories, and concepts to improve district operations.				
	b. Demonstrate an understanding of the complex causes of poverty and other disadvantages and their effects on families, communities, children, and learning.				
	c. Demonstrate an understanding of the policies, laws, and regulations enacted by local, state, and federal authorities affecting a particular district.				
	d. Explain the system for financing public schools and its effects on the equitable distribution of educational opportunities within a district.				
	e. Demonstrate the ability to work with political leaders at the local, state, and national level.				
	f. Apply an understanding of how specific laws at the local, state, and federal level affect school districts and residents.				
	g. Espouse positions in response to proposed policy changes that would benefit or harm districts and explain how proposed policies and laws might improve educational and social opportunities for specific communities.				

6.2 Respond to the Larger Context	a. Demonstrate the ability to engage students, parents, members of the school board, and other community members in advocating for adoption of improved policies and laws.				
	b. Apply their understanding of the larger political, social, economic, legal, and cultural context to develop activities and policies that benefit their district and its students.				
	c. Demonstrate the ability to communicate regularly with all segments of the district community concerning trends, issues, and policies affecting the district.				
6.3 Influence the Larger Context	a. Demonstrate an understanding of how to develop lines of communication with local, state, and federal authorities and actively advocate for improved policies, laws, and regulations affecting a specific district, both directly and through organizations representing schools, educators, or others with similar interests.				
	b. Demonstrate the ability to advocate for policies and programs that promote equitable learning opportunities and success for all students, regardless of socioeconomic background, ethnicity, gender, disability, or other individual characteristics.				

Ways for You to Do It:

A superintendent leader can enhance systematic school improvement by using the following strategies:

- Being visible and maintaining open channels of communication
- Keeping politics and personal sentiment from impacting student education
- Implementing and utilizing a chain-of-command policy that has been collaboratively developed by multiple stakeholders in the school community
- Not being afraid to take a stand on difficult issues
- Maintaining professionalism and good public relations, even when solidly against an issue
- Staying current on all concerns that could impact your district and student education, including state and federal legislation, financial models, and societal issues
- Being actively involved in state and other external funding procurement
- Treating all employees equally without giving preferential treatment to friends or family and avoiding even the appearance of nepotism
- Doing what needs to be done behind closed doors while in public supporting your staff
- Leading the collaborative development of emergency and media plans
- Being proactive by seeking to put out fires before they get out of hand
- Being fair and just
- Facilitating conflict resolution training for all employees and participating in it yourself
- Remembering that you are *first* a teacher, with a role of teaching the public the basic things they need to understand in regard to the appropriateness of a free and appropriate education for all students regardless of their circumstances, language, or special needs.

CONCLUSIONS

The days are gone when school superintendents could operate their districts in a vacuum as a single unit apart from others. Today's school districts have become collaborative entities with local, state, and federal agencies and in alliance with other school districts, families, community groups, and social agencies. Never has there been a time when the words "no man is an island" have been more true than in district leadership today. With increasing student populations; more diversity; complex causes and consequences of poverty; and vast differences among peoples, cultures, and learning styles, it is essential that we seek to maximize all our constituencies' understanding of, responses to, and influences of political, social, economic, legal, and cultural entities for the joint goal of improving education for all students.

The Ultimate Application

The following questions are designed to assist you in applying higher-level thinking skills through application. Either alone or in a group setting respond to each question based upon your own knowledge, experience, and further research.

1. Define and provide examples of the superintendent's role in incorporating political, social, economic, legal, and cultural contexts in district leadership.

2. Describe the community's perception of your district based on knowledge of how you and the school board address the political, social, economic, legal, and cultural aspects of facilitating student success.

3. Develop a plan and time line of the things you as superintendent can do to be more directly and indirectly involved in student and family advocacy within a free and democratic society.

4. Describe a framework by which you could facilitate faculty, staff, and other learning-community members in becoming advocates for student success within political, social, economic, legal, and cultural contexts.

5. Define and explain *social justice.* Develop activities for your administrators to participate in and lead that expand the development of social justice systems within your school district.

6. Select a topic of potential controversy from within your school district. Prepare pros and cons for each side of the position based on researched data, policy, law, and other relevant factors for the contextual situation. Develop a position paper and make recommendations based on the data gathered.

7. Identify and develop activities that could be done within the school district that utilize the skills of the learning community relating to current or potential trends that could impact change in the learning environment.

The Superintendent Internship

"Surround yourself with only people who are going to lift you higher."

—Oprah Winfrey

> **Standard 7:** The internship provides significant opportunities for candidates to synthesize and apply the knowledge and practice and develop the skills identified in Standards 1–6 through substantial, sustained, standards-based work in real settings, planned and guided cooperatively by the institution and school district personnel for graduate credit

INTRODUCTION

The following case description is an example of how one university utilized Standard 7 in the development and implementation of a superintendent certification plan. While providing a sample implementation model, it is not presented here as a template on which all programs should be modeled. Rather, it is provided to help you visualize one way Standard 7 can be utilized and to encourage discussion in university program development arenas.

In response to Dallas-Fort Worth metropolitan area needs, Dallas Baptist University has collaboratively developed a doctor of education degree in educational leadership. The program has three tracks:

1. Higher Education Leadership
2. K–12 Education Leadership
3. Ministry Education Leadership

Doctoral students take core research and other subjects together. Each track subsequently has its own courses designed to meet specific learner-centered objectives. All students have rich, meaningful, and substantial opportunities in real settings to participate in multiple integrated activities, such as trips to Washington, D.C., and South Korea for doctoral credit at university expense. Significant and specific required doctoral courses are offered on these trips, which integrate field experiences with the knowledge, skills, and dispositions necessary to become effective educational leaders. In conjunction with the university mission, all courses are designed to integrate faith and learning, to incorporate service learning, and to develop and enhance servant leaders. Each track includes a year-long internship for doctoral credit that is planned, implemented, and evaluated jointly with the university and the arena in which the internship is taking place. This chapter will focus on the K–12 track, which is an excellent example of a superintendency program that is substantial, sustained, and standards based. Each internship is in a real setting, is planned and guided cooperatively between the university and the appropriate field placement, lasts for two semesters, and is worth 6 hours of doctoral credit.

As shown in Figure 8.1, there are five core concepts that are critical to the implementation superintendent internships.

Figure 8.1   Standards-Based Internships

Standards-Based Superintendent Internships Are

- Substantial;
- Sustained;
- Standards based;
- In real settings;
- Planned and guided cooperatively; and
- For graduate credit.

Source: Dayton & Jenni Barone

SUBSTANTIAL

For a superintendent internship to be defined as "substantial," students should be able to demonstrate the ability to accept genuine responsibility for leading, facilitating, and making decisions typical of those made by district leaders. The interns should be provided opportunities to work on important projects and use concepts that will prepare them for an upper-level district leadership position. The scope and responsibilities necessary to complete these tasks should increase in complexity, higher-level thinking, and application skills as the internship progresses. Interns should have direct opportunities to work and be involved with district staff, the school board, students, parents, and both school and community leaders (Bjork & Kowalski, 2005; Cambron-McCabe, 2005; Fusarelli & Fusarelli, 2005).

In an ideal world, each intern would be able to have a full-time internship that lasts at least six months. The definition of *full time* is correlated to the requirement for federal financial aid, which is usually 9–12 hours per week. Interns at Dallas Baptist University are required to enroll in K–12 District Internship for a total of 6 graduate hours (two 3-hour courses) over two semesters. They are required to complete a minimum of 250 hours per course for a total of 500 standards-based hours in directly related superintendent experiences. The two internship courses may be taken in any combination of fall, spring, and long-summer semesters.

SUSTAINED

For a program to be considered "sustained," the interns must work with their university supervisor as well as their district supervisor(s) to plan and implement projects that will have a district improvement impact spanning the entire internship experience. Activities should include opportunities, particularly near the end of the experience, for interns to apply their knowledge and skills on a full-time basis as defined above.

Superintendent interns at Dallas Baptist University develop a complex Professional Portfolio over the course of their two-semester internship experience. Their Professional Portfolio contains their educational leadership philosophy; their internship goals; and their plans for achieving them, which they have jointly developed with their university and field supervisor(s). It also contains designs, standards-aligned logs, and artifacts of how they achieved standards-based experiences throughout the two semesters; evidence of extensive utilization of technology; and copies of their doctoral transcript and their university degree audit, including their state certification plans. More than documentation of standards-based internship activities, the Professional Portfolios are designed to be ongoing, living documents that interns can modify and enhance throughout their careers as their experiences evolve. The goal is to provide a mechanism for students to be able to authenticate being learners, not simply during their internship experience but for the rest of their lives.

STANDARDS-BASED

Internships should be individually planned to fulfill the needs of each student. Likewise, experiences should be planned and implemented based on individual state standards. If a state does not have a specific, targeted set of standards for district-level leadership, the ELCC standards described in this book are an excellent set to utilize. By the end of the internship experience, each student should know, understand, and be able to apply the standards for improved personal, school, and district performance.

Students in the K–12 District Leadership track at Dallas Baptist University utilize the standards (3 domains and 10 competencies) as prescribed by the Texas legislature in Texas Education Code (2006). These domains and competencies, shown below, are remarkably similar to the ELCC standards.

Domain I—Leadership of the Educational Community

- *Competency 001:* The superintendent knows how to act with integrity, fairness, and in an ethical manner in order to promote the success of all students.
- *Competency 002:* The superintendent knows how to shape district culture by facilitating the development, articulation, implementation, and stewardship of a vision of learning that is shared and supported by the educational community.
- *Competency 003:* The superintendent knows how to communicate and collaborate with families and community members, respond to diverse community interests and needs, and mobilize community resources to ensure educational success for all students.
- *Competency 004:* The superintendent knows how to respond to and influence the larger political, social, economic, legal, and cultural context, including working with the board of trustees, to achieve the district's educational vision.

Domain II—Instructional Leadership

- *Competency 005:* The superintendent knows how to facilitate the planning and implementation of strategic plans that enhance teaching and learning; ensure alignment among curriculum, curriculum resources, and assessment; and promote the use of varied assessments to measure student performance.

- *Competency 006:* The superintendent knows how to advocate, nurture, and sustain an instructional program and a district culture that are conducive to student learning and staff professional growth.
- *Competency 007:* The superintendent knows how to implement a staff evaluation and development system to improve the performance of all staff members and select appropriate models for supervision and staff development.

Domain III—Administrative Leadership

- *Competency 008:* The superintendent knows how to apply principles of effective leadership and management in relation to district budgeting, personnel, resource utilization, financial management, and technology use.
- *Competency 009:* The superintendent knows how to apply principles of leadership and management to the district's physical plan and support systems to ensure a safe and effective learning environment.
- *Competency 010:* The superintendent knows how to apply organizational, decision-making, and problem-solving skills to facilitate positive change in varied contexts. (Texas Education Code [2006])

All persons wishing to become public district superintendents in the State of Texas are required to pass a difficult state certification examination called the Texas Examination of Educator Standards (TExES). More information can be found at the following Web sites:

- *Texas Examinations of Educator Standards Preparation Manual (Superintendent):* www.texes.ets.org/assets/pdf/testprep_manuals/ 064_superintendent_55069_web.pdf
- *Texas Examinations of Educator Standards Preparation Manual (Superintendent: District Profile Packet):* www.texes.ets.org/assets/ pdf/testprep_manuals/064_superintendent2.pdf

As shown in Figure 8.2, the TExES domains and competencies are directly aligned with the ELCC standards.

Each university and alternative educational provider is scored by the state on how well its students do on these tests. If students from any demographic subgroup do not score well, a university or alternative educational provider can lose its state authorization to offer educator certification in any field. This includes all certifications from initial teacher credentialing, additional teaching, or leading fields and includes the superintendency. Therefore, providing students quality, standards-based knowledge and application skills is of significant importance to all Texas universities. Dallas Baptist University prides itself on the high quality of

Figure 8.2 Alignment of ELCC Standards With TExES Domains and Competencies

	ELCC Standard 1	ELCC Standard 2	ELCC Standard 3	ELCC Standard 4	ELCC Standard 5	ELCC Standard 6	ELCC Standard 7
TExES 001					√+		√
TExES 002	√+						√
TExES 003				√+			√
TExES 004						√+	√
TExES 005		√+					√
TExES 006		√+					√
TExES 007		√+					√
TExES 008			√			√	√
TExES 009			√+				√
TExES 010	√			√			√

√+ = Primary Focus of Standard   √ = Addressed in Standard

teachers, principals, and superintendents who complete their programs. Graduates do well on both these difficult standards-based tests and their performance in the field in real settings.

REAL SETTINGS

It is important that future superintendents have more than knowledge learned in coursework through texts and other resources. They must be able to move from a knowledge base to an application base. This is done by providing students opportunities to learn and perform in authentic district settings. The ideal internship would arrange for the student to have experience in diverse settings rather than having all experiences in the same building, location, or specialization area (curriculum, instruction, finance, facilities management, etc.). Superintendents need to be able to apply their skills in all aspects of this top leadership role. The specifics for these application skills are delineated in the ELCC standards and many state standards, such as those described above for the State of Texas.

In addition, interns need to have opportunities to work with many different internal and external district groups. This includes civic and parent groups within the community as well as with their own school board. Interns need an opportunity to spread their wings as representatives of the district while still having a strong district and university support system, as they are just learning to fly.

To this end, all Dallas Baptist University educational leadership internships (superintendent, principal, higher education, and ministry) are accomplished in actual field settings within the proper arena. Thus, the superintendent internship is done in varied sites and contexts at a school district's top level of leadership. In addition to real settings, Dallas Baptist University seeks to provide students with opportunities to expand their understanding of policy into actual practice within individual courses. During the summer of 2006, educational leadership doctoral students had the opportunity to travel to Washington, D.C., at university expense to see policy, legislation, and historical leadership concepts in practice. Students enrolled in the K–12 Education Leadership track registered for a course called Learning Communities. Course goals and objectives were achieved by time spent in class in Washington, D.C., but, more so, by students having opportunities over a week's time to visit with Senator Kay Bailey Hutchison and Congressman Kenny Marchant, both representing Texas, as well as visit the House of Representatives while it was in session; tour the capitol; have a private orientation within the Supreme Court; visit the Smithsonian; take in a private lecture and tour of the U.S. Naval Academy at Annapolis, Maryland; enjoy reserved seating and a private tour of the National Cathedral, the Tomb of the Unknown Soldier, the Holocaust Museum, and the Library of Congress; and visit with leaders at the headquarters of the American Association of School Administrators (AASA) among other experiences. It was a full, exhausting, and exhilarating week as students got to tie theory and policy to actual leadership practice within the nation's capitol. During the summer of 2007, students had a similar opportunity, again at university expense, to visit and learn international educational and leadership strategies at schools in South Korea.

PLANNED AND GUIDED COOPERATIVELY

Internship experiences should be planned collaboratively by the individual, the site supervisor, and the university to include multiple opportunities to use the standards-based knowledge, skills, and research the student has studied. Internships should be individually planned so each student gets the application opportunities that address individual strengths and weaknesses. Throughout the internship, each student should be mentored and supported to maximize learning opportunities and applications.

Continuing with the Dallas Baptist University illustration, interns in the superintendency program develop this plan during the first semester of their two-semester internship. Specific time lines and strategies are jointly determined to provide a realistic plan to achieve the student's goals and to manage the student's time most appropriately. Projects are developed and broken into smaller components, and necessary resources are identified jointly by the intern, the site supervisor(s), and the university supervisor. There is a dual goal of providing the interns opportunities to utilize learning opportunities as well as helping the district target, implement, and accomplish something it needs done but, for whatever reasons, has not been able to achieve.

An application of this has occurred at Dallas Baptist University, where a group of one professor and three EdD superintendent students developed a close alliance with the Educational Region Service Center 10 located in Richardson, Texas. Under the joint direction of the region service center special education coordinator, Ellen Kimbrough, and this professor, Dallas Baptist University doctoral students Amy Burkman, Gloria Key, and Kaye Tindell worked to develop the content for a Service Center Web site defining and linking scientifically based research for special education K–12 teachers and directors for language arts, math, science, social studies, and fine arts. This mammoth project was accomplished by the collaborative efforts of each person working both independently and together. Regularly scheduled meetings were held at the Service Center in Richardson, at the university, and at sites in between to save driving time for the individual stakeholders. Dallas Baptist University displayed its support of this vast research project with the campus welcome sign shown in Figure 8.3.

This research-based Web site is under final construction at this book's press time. You can take a look at it here: www.region10.org/specialeducation/sbr.html. It will be one of the first of its kind not just to include scientifically based research but to identify specific strategies per content area, link to appropriate resources, and provide the research to substantiate that they are, indeed, scientifically based.

GRADUATE CREDIT

Interns should receive graduate credit for their internship experiences. At Dallas Baptist University, interns receive doctoral credit of 3 hours each

Figure 8.3   Scientifically Based Research Sign at Dallas Baptist University

Source: Photo by G. C. Key

for the two-semester internship for a total of 6 hours of credit. These internship requirements are required elements for both their degree and state certification plans as developed by the university and approved by the Texas State Board for Educator Certification (SBEC).

ASSESSMENT MODEL

Standard 7: The internship provides significant opportunities for candidates to synthesize and apply the knowledge and practice and develop the skills identified in Standards 1–6 through substantial, sustained, standards-based work in real settings, planned and guided cooperatively by the institution and school district personnel for graduate credit.

In Table 8.1, you will find a planning rubric for assessing your program's progress toward this standard. Vertical and horizontal mentoring are important elements in maximizing your program's success. For additional reading on administrator induction and mentoring, see *Principal Induction: A Standards-Based Model for Administrator Development* (Wilmore, 2004).

Table 8.1   Planning Rubric for Standard 7

Element	Goals to Meet Standard for Improved School District Leadership Preparation	Specific Activities Designed to Achieve Standard	People and Resources Needed to Operationalize This Strategy	Date by Which Activity Will Be Completed	Evidence of Standard Attainment
7.1 Substantial	a. Demonstrate the ability to accept genuine responsibility for leading, facilitating, and making decisions typical of those made by district leaders. The experience(s) should provide interns with substantial responsibilities that increase over time in amount and complexity and involve direct interaction and involvement with staff, school board members, students, parents, and school and community leaders.				
	b. Have a maximum of six months (or equivalent, see * below) of full-time internship experience.				
7.2 Sustained	a. Participate in planned intern activities during the entire course of the program, including an extended period of time near the conclusion of the program, to allow candidate to apply skills and knowledge on a full-time basis.				
7.3 Standards-based	a. Apply skills and knowledge articulated in these standards as well as state and local standards for educational leaders.				
	b. Experiences are designed to accommodate candidates' individual needs.				

126

7.4 Real Settings	a. Experiences occur in multiple district administrator settings and allow for the demonstration of relevant knowledge and skills.				
	b. Experiences include work with appropriate community organizations, parent groups, and school boards.				
7.5 Planned and Guided Cooperatively	a. Experiences are planned cooperatively by the individual, the site supervisor, and institution personnel to include appropriate opportunities to apply skills, knowledge, and research contained in the standards. These individuals work together to meet candidate and program needs.				
	b. Mentors are provided training to guide the candidate during the intern experience.				
7.6 Credit	a. Candidates earn graduate credit for their intern experience.				

* The six-month internship experience need not be consecutive and may include experiences of different lengths. However, all internships must include an extended, capstone experience to maximize the candidates' opportunities to practice and refine their skills and knowledge. This culminating experience may be two noncontiguous internships of three months each, a four-month internship and two field practicums of one month each, or another equivalent combination. *Full-time experience* is defined as the number of hours per week required for attendance by a full-time student receiving federal financial assistance (generally 9–12 hours per week).

CONCLUSIONS

Universities, alternative educational providers, and school districts must work together collaboratively to plan, implement, and evaluate superintendent internship experiences that will authentically provide students with the learning opportunities they need to be successful district leaders. The internship activities must be substantial in nature, designed to help them apply and evaluate their knowledge, skills, and dispositions in a meaningful and relevant way. This cannot happen unless the district, university, and student work together to plan and guide the learning experience in a variety of administrative settings. Activities should be based on state standards or the Educational Leadership Constituent Council Standards. Often, state standards are already aligned with the ELCC or the Interstate School Leaders Licensure Consortium (ISLLC) standards. These standards-based activities should be sustained over a period of time and integrated throughout the superintendent program. They should also include an opportunity for the student to apply learnings on a full-time basis at or near the end of the program. Students also should receive graduate credit for their internship.

When each stakeholder—the universities, alternative educational preparation programs, school districts, and the students themselves—work together to plan and implement maximized, standards-based learning activities with significant formative and summative feedback and consistent mentoring, the superintendents of tomorrow will be best prepared to meet the vastly changing and diverse needs of school districts of the future. To each entity that is working on a day-to-day basis to provide these learning opportunities, our applause goes to you. You are providing the "soft pillow" upon which interns can be allowed to fall when things go wrong. When they fall, we are there to mentor, nurture, sustain, support, and challenge them to become all they can be for the districts of today and tomorrow. Anything less is not good enough.

The Ultimate Application

The following questions are designed to assist you in applying higher-level thinking skills through application. Either alone or in a group setting respond to each question based upon your own knowledge, experience, and further research.

1. What are ways that you as superintendent can initiate discussions with a university for a collaborative internship program to be developed and implemented in your district?

2. Would you, or would you not, allow current administrators to have release time to fulfill the requirements of a year-long internship? Substantiate your answer.

3. Define ways you would ensure that the year-long internship in your district was substantial and of significant value in the learning process of the intern.

4. Describe ways you could make sure superintendent interns in your district receive a sustained application of their knowledge, skills, and dispositions.

5. Discuss your personal perceptions of standards-based education and how this model could impact superintendent interns working in your district. Compare and contrast any benefits, or liabilities, you see in regard to a standards-based internship.

6. How would you go about ensuring that a superintendent intern in your district has the opportunity to learn and serve in more than one district leadership capacity?

7. Describe ways in which you could work collaboratively with a university or alternative education provider to plan and guide a superintendent internship to guarantee the intern has opportunities to learn, grow, and be mentored in appropriate district-level leadership skills.

It's Up to You

"One shoe can change your life."

—Cinderella

FINAL APPLICATIONS

Throughout *Superintendent Leadership*, we have sought to dig deep into the meaning and application of the Educational Leadership Constituent Council standards. We have learned that superintendents are educational leaders who have the knowledge and ability to promote the success of all students by using the following strategies:

- Facilitating the development, articulation, implementation, and stewardship of a school or district vision of learning supported by the school community (Standard 1)
- Promoting a positive school culture, providing an effective instructional program, applying best practices to student learning, and designing comprehensive professional growth plans for staff (Standard 2)
- Managing the organization, operations, and resources in a way that promotes a safe, efficient, and effective learning environment (Standard 3)
- Collaborating with families and other community members, responding to diverse community interests and needs, and mobilizing community resources (Standard 4)
- Acting with integrity, fairly, and in an ethical manner (Standard 5)

- Understanding, responding to, and influencing the larger political, social, economic, legal, and cultural context (Standard 6)
- Having had an internship that provides significant opportunities for candidates to synthesize and apply the knowledge and practice and develop the skills identified in Standards 1–6 through substantial, sustained, standards-based work in real settings, planned and guided cooperatively by the institution and school district personnel for graduate credit (Standard 7)

None of this happens in isolation. Superintendents integrate their knowledge, skills, and dispositions from each of these standards into their day-to-day leadership roles without stopping to think, "Gee, is what I am doing now something I learned in Standard 1 or Standard 5?" The pieces of the world do not exist in isolation. Leadership surely does not. All learning must be applied and integrated into a global composite that encompasses the total gestalt of your leadership philosophy, style, and application.

RECOMMENDATIONS

The rest is up to you. You have learned in detail what each of the standards means. You have been provided with examples, case studies, applications, an assessment model to use to measure your own growth, and reflective activities. How you use what you have learned is a personal decision directly connected to your desire to be a lifelong learner. I sincerely hope that you will use these ELCC standards for the function for which they were developed: to help you become the best superintendent you can possibly be. Remember, they are not rules. They are guidelines and benchmarks by which you can measure your progress toward being the Ideal Superintendent who works hard every day to meet the needs of every student, regardless of that student's circumstances.

GO FORTH, AND DO WELL!

After working your way through this book and reflectively reading, pondering, and analyzing your own experiences in light of those described in the ELCC standards, you may feel that it would take a Super Superintendent to do all of these things. As a mere mortal, you may feel that you'll be able to walk on water before accomplishing these standards.

Do not let these high standards stop you from trying to achieve them. Move to the top! Be positive! Be proactive! Focus on the needs of the students in your district. Keep your eyes and ears open while searching within the grassroots and the learning community. Be a good listener. Really hear what people are telling you about the needs and concerns in the trenches. Be the People's Superintendent who is relentless in search for equity and displays integrity, caring, and compassion toward those in need. Be the superintendent that others want you to be.

For that, folks, is what the ELCC standards were developed to enable. You become the superintendent whom others look to as ideal. You become the one who never gives up in the relentless pursuit of perfection. You lead the way. Let others follow you. Remember, one shoe can change your life.

In doing so, I hope your career is blessed beyond all measure and that you never, ever stop moving forward and making the world a better place for children, families, and society now and forever.

Suggested Additional Reading

This list is not intended to be an exhaustive guide but rather a source of supplemental reading that supports the concepts presented in the ELCC standards. Many of these resources include content that is relevant to more than one standard.

Standard 1

Bennis, W. (1989). *Why leaders can't lead.* San Francisco: Jossey-Bass.

Blanchard, K., & Bowles, S. (1998). *Gung-ho!* New York: William Morrow.

Blanchard, K., Hybels, B., & Hodges, P. (1999). *Leadership by the book: Tools to transform your workplace.* New York: William Morrow.

Bolman, L. G., & Deal, T. E. (1997). *Reframing organizations: Artistry, choice, and leadership* (2nd ed.). San Francisco: Jossey-Bass.

Bolman, L. G., & Deal, T. E. (2001). *Leading with soul: An uncommon journey of spirit.* San Francisco: Jossey-Bass.

Bolman, L. G., & Deal, T. E. (2002). *Reframing the path to school leadership: A guide for teachers and principals.* Thousand Oaks, CA: Corwin Press.

Brock, B. L., & Grady, M. L. (2000). *Rekindling the flame.* Thousand Oaks, CA: Corwin Press.

Brower, R. E., & Balch, B. V. (2005). *Transformational leadership & decision making in schools.* Thousand Oaks, CA: Corwin Press.

Deal, T. E., & Bolman, L. G. (2001). *Leading with soul.* San Francisco, CA: Jossey-Bass.

De Pree, M. (1989). *Leadership is an art.* New York: Dell.

Developing a framework for the continual professional development of administrators in the northeast: DeWitt Wallace-Reader's Digest Fund Study Conference. (1992). Andover, MA: Regional Laboratory for Educational Improvement of the Northeast & Islands. (ERIC Document Reproduction Service No. ED383104)

Dickmann, M. H., & Stanford-Blair, N. (2002). *Connecting leadership to the brain.* Thousand Oaks, CA: Corwin Press.

Dyer, K. M., & Carothers, J. (2000). *The intuitive principal.* Thousand Oaks, CA: Corwin Press.

Eisner, E. W. (2005). *Reimagining schools: The selected works of Elliot W. Eisner.* Florence, KY: Routledge.

Elias, M. J., Arnold, H., & Steiger Hussey, C. (Eds.). (2002). *EQ + IQ = Best leadership practices for caring.* Thousand Oaks, CA: Corwin Press.

Fullan, M. (2001). *Leading in a culture of change.* San Francisco: Jossey-Bass.

Fullan, M. (2004). *Leadership & sustainability: System thinkers in action.* Thousand Oaks, CA: Corwin Press.

Hoyle, J. (2001). *Leadership and the force of love: Six keys to motivating with love.* Thousand Oaks, CA: Corwin Press.

Hoyle, J. (2006). *Leadership and futuring: Making visions happen* (2nd ed.). Thousand Oaks, CA: Corwin Press.

Johnson, S. (1998). *Who moved my cheese?* New York: Putnam.

Kouzes, J. M., & Posner, B. Z. (1998). *Encouraging the heart: A leader's guide to rewarding and recognizing others.* San Francisco: Jossey-Bass.

Krzyzewski, M., & Phillips, D. T. (2000). *Leading with the heart: Coach K's successful strategies for basketball, business, and life.* New York: Warner Business Books.

Louis, K. S. (2005). *Organizing for school change.* Florence, KY: Routledge.

Lovely, S. (2005). *Setting leadership priorities: What's necessary, what's nice, and what's got to go.* Thousand Oaks, CA: Corwin Press.

MacKay, L. L., & Ralston, E. W. (1999). *Creating better schools.* Thousand Oaks, CA: Corwin Press.

Maxwell, J. C. (1995). *Developing the leaders around you.* Nashville, TN: Thomas Nelson.

Murphy, J. F., & Datnow, A. (Eds.). (2002). *Leadership lessons from comprehensive school reforms.* Thousand Oaks, CA: Corwin Press.

Peters, T., & Waterman, R. H. (1993). *In search of excellence.* New York: Warner Books.

Ramsey, R. D. (1999). *Lead, follow, or get out of the way.* Thousand Oaks, CA: Corwin Press.

Sergiovanni, T. J. (1990). *Value-added leadership: How to get extraordinary performance in schools.* Orlando, FL: Harcourt Brace Jovanovich.

Sergiovanni, T. J. (2001). *The principalship: A reflective practice perspective* (4th ed.). Needham Heights, MA: Allyn & Bacon.

Sharp, W. L., Walter, J. K., & Sharp, H. M. (1998). *Case studies for school leaders: Implementing the ISLLC standards.* Lancaster, PA: Technomic.

Sparks, D. (2006). *Leading for results: Transforming teaching, learning, and relationships in schools* (2nd ed.). Thousand Oaks, CA: Corwin Press.

Spears, L., Lawrence, M., & Blanchard, K. (2002). *Focus on leadership: Servant-leadership for the 21st century.* New York: John Wiley & Sons, Inc.

Williams, R. B. (2006). *More than 50 ways to build team consensus* (2nd ed.). Thousand Oaks, CA: Corwin Press.

Standard 2

Ardovino, J., Hollingsworth, J., & Ybarra, S. (2000). *Multiple measures: Accurate ways to assess student achievement.* Thousand Oaks, CA: Corwin Press.

Arter, J., & McTighe, J. (2001). *Scoring rubrics in the classroom: Using performance criteria for assessing and improving student performance.* Thousand Oaks, CA: Corwin Press.

Banks, J. A. (2006). *Race, culture, and education: The selected works of James A. Banks.* Florence, KY: Routledge.

Banks, J. A., & Banks, C. M. (1996). *Multicultural education: Issues and perspectives.* Boston: Allyn & Bacon.

Barker, C. L., & Searchwell, C. J. (2001). *Writing year-end teacher improvement plans—right now!!* Thousand Oaks, CA: Corwin Press.

Barker, C. L., & Searchwell, C. J. (2003). *Writing meaningful teacher evaluations— right now!!* (2nd ed.). Thousand Oaks, CA: Corwin Press.

Barth, R. S. (2003). *Lessons learned: Shaping relationships and the culture of the workplace.* Thousand Oaks, CA: Corwin Press.

Beach, D. M., & Reinhartz, J. (2000). *Supervisory leadership.* Boston: Allyn & Bacon.

Beane, J. A. (1997). *Curriculum integration: Designing the core of democratic education.* New York: Teachers College Press.

Bigge, M. L., & Shermis, S. S. (1999). *Learning theories for teachers* (6th ed.). New York: Addison-Wesley Longman.

Blanchard, K., & Johnson, S. (1981). *The one minute manager.* New York: Berkley.

Blankstein, A. M. (2004). *Failure is not an option: Six principles that guide student achievement in high-performing schools.* Thousand Oaks, CA: Corwin Press.

Blase, J., & Kirby, P. C. (1999). *Bringing out the best in teachers: What effective principals do* (2nd ed.). Thousand Oaks, CA: Corwin Press.

Bocchino, R. (1999). *Emotional literacy: To be a different kind of smart.* Thousand Oaks, CA: Corwin Press.

Bolman, L. G., & Deal, T. E. (2002). *Reframing the path to school leadership: A guide for teachers and principals.* Thousand Oaks, CA: Corwin Press.

Bracey, G. W. (2000). *Bail me out! Handling difficult data and tough questions about public schools.* Thousand Oaks, CA: Corwin Press.

Brewer, E. W., DeJonge, J. O., & Stout, V. J. (2001). *Moving online: Making the transition from traditional instruction and communication strategies.* Thousand Oaks, CA: Corwin Press.

Brock, B. L., & Grady, M. L. (2007). *From first-year to first-rate: Principals guiding beginning teachers* (3rd ed.). Thousand Oaks, CA: Corwin Press.

Bucher, R. D. (2000). *Diversity consciousness: Opening our minds to people, cultures, and opportunities.* Upper Saddle River, NJ: Prentice Hall.

Burrello, L. C., Lashley, C., & Beatty, E. E. (2001). *Educating all students together: How school leaders create unified systems.* Thousand Oaks, CA: Corwin Press.

Burton, V. R. (2000). *Rich minds, rich rewards.* Dallas, TX: Pearl.

Carbo, M. (2000). *What every principal should know about teaching reading.* Syosset, NY: National Reading Styles Institute.

Chapman, C., & Gregory, G. H. (2006). *Differential instructional strategies: One size doesn't fit all* (2nd ed.). Thousand Oaks, CA: Corwin Press.

Costa, A. L., & Garmston, R. J. (1994). *Cognitive coaching.* Norwood, MA: Christopher Gordon.

Creighton, T. B. (2006). *Schools and data: The educator's guide for using data to improve decision making* (2nd ed.). Thousand Oaks, CA: Corwin Press.

Crow, G. M., & Matthews, L. J. (1998). *Finding one's way: How mentoring can lead to dynamic leadership.* Thousand Oaks, CA: Corwin Press.

Cuttance, P. (2006). *An evidence-based approach to school innovation and improvement.* Florence, KY: Routledge.

Danielson, C., & McGreal, T. L. (2000). *Teacher evaluation to enhance professional practice.* Princeton, NJ: Educational Testing Service.

Daresh, J. C. (2001). *Leaders helping leaders: A practical guide to administrative mentoring* (2nd ed.). Thousand Oaks, CA: Corwin Press.

Daresh, J. C. (2002). *Teachers mentoring teachers: A practical approach to helping new and experienced staff.* Thousand Oaks, CA: Corwin Press.

Deal, T. E., & Peterson, K. D. (1994). *The leadership paradox.* San Francisco: Jossey-Bass.

Deal, T. E., & Peterson, K. D. (1999). *Shaping school culture: The heart of leadership.* San Francisco: Jossey-Bass.

Deli'Olio, J., & Donk, T. (2007). *Models of teaching: Connecting student learning with standards.* Thousand Oaks, CA: Sage Publications.

Denmark, V. M., & Podsen, I. J. (2000). *Coaching and mentoring first-year and student teachers.* Larchmont, NY: Eye on Education.

Earl, L. M., & Katz, S. (2006). *Leading schools in a data-rich world: Harnessing data for school improvement.* Thousand Oaks, CA: Corwin Press.

English, F. W. (2000). *Deciding what to teach and test: Developing, aligning, and auditing the curriculum* (millennium ed.). Thousand Oaks, CA: Corwin Press.

Erickson, L. H. (2002). *Concept-based curriculum and instruction: Teaching beyond the facts.* Thousand Oaks, CA: Corwin Press.

Glanz, J. (1998). *Action research: An educational guide to school improvement.* Norwood, MA: Christopher Gordan.

Glatthorn, A. A. (2001). *The principal as curriculum leader* (2nd ed.). Thousand Oaks, CA: Corwin Press.

Glatthorn, A. A., Boshcee, F., & Whitehead, B. M. (2006). *Curriculum leadership: Development and implementation.* Thousand Oaks, CA: Sage.

Glenn, H. S., & Brock, M. L. (1998). *7 strategies for developing capable students.* Roseville, CA: Prima.

Gregory, G. H., & Chapman, C. (2006). *Differentiated instructional strategies: One size doesn't fit all* (2nd ed.). Thousand Oaks, CA: Corwin Press.

Hadaway, N., Vardell, S. M., & Young, T. (2001). *Literature-based instruction with English language learners.* Boston: Allyn & Bacon.

Henze, R. C., Katz, A., Norte, E., Sather. S. E., & Walker, E. (2002). *Leading for diversity: How school leaders promote interethnic relations.* Thousand Oaks, CA: Corwin Press.

Holcomb, E. L. (2004). *Getting excited about data: How to combine people, passion, and proof to maximize student achievement* (2nd ed.). Thousand Oaks, CA: Corwin Press.

Holt, L. C., & Kysika, M. L. (2006). *Instructional patterns: Strategies for maximizing student learning.* Thousand Oaks, CA: Sage.

Hoyle, J. H., English, F., & Steffy, B. (1998). *Skills for successful 21st century school leaders.* Arlington, VA: American Association of School Administrators.

Johnson, R. S. (2002). *Using data to close the achievement gap: How to measure equity in our schools.* Thousand Oaks, CA: Corwin Press.

Joyce, B., & Weil, M. (1996). *Models of teaching.* Needham Heights, MA: Simon & Schuster.

Joyner, E. T., Ben-Avie, M., & Comer, J. P. (2004). *Transforming school leadership and management to support student learning and development: The field guide to Comer schools in action.* Thousand Oaks, CA: Corwin Press.

Kennedy, E. (2003). *Raising test scores for all students: An administrator's guide to improving standardized test performance.* Thousand Oaks, CA: Corwin Press.

Kimmelman, P. L. (2006). *Implementing NCLB: Creating a knowledge framework to support school improvement.* Thousand Oaks, CA: Corwin Press.

Kirby, P. C., & Blase, J. (2000). *Bringing out the best in teachers: What effective principals do* (2nd ed.). Thousand Oaks, CA: Corwin Press.

Kozol, J. (1992). *Savage inequalities: Children in America's schools.* New York: Harper Perennial Library.

Kozol, J. (2000). *Ordinary resurrections: Children in the years of hope.* New York: Crown Press.

Leithwood, K., Aitken, R., & Jantzi, D. (2006). *Making schools smarter: Leading with evidence* (3rd ed.). Thousand Oaks, CA: Corwin Press.

Marlowe, B. A., & Page, M. L. (2005). *Creating and sustaining the constructivist classroom* (2nd ed.). Thousand Oaks, CA: Corwin Press.

Monahan, T. (2005). *Globalization, technological change, and public education.* Florence, KY: Routledge.

Moore, K. (2005). *Effective instructional strategies: From theory to practice.* Thousand Oaks, CA: Sage.

Moxley, D. E., & Taylor, R. T. (2006). *Literacy coaching: A handbook for school leaders.* Thousand Oaks, CA: Corwin Press.

Nielsen, L. B. (2002). *Brief reference of student disabilities . . . with strategies for the classroom.* Thousand Oaks, CA: Corwin Press.

Obiakor, F. E., & Ford, B. A. (2002). *Creating successful learning environments for African American learners with exceptionalities.* Thousand Oaks, CA: Corwin Press.

Oliva, P. F. (1997). *Supervision in today's schools* (5th ed.). New York: John Wiley.

Payne, R. K. (2003). *A framework for understanding poverty* (3rd rev. ed.). Highlands, TX: Aha! Process.

Peterson, K. D. (2002). *Effective teacher hiring: A guide to getting the best.* Alexandria, VA: Association for Supervision & Curriculum Development.

Podsen, I. J. (2002). *Teacher retention: What is your weakest link?* Larchmont, NY: Eye on Education.

Pratt, D. (1994) *Curriculum planning: A handbook for professionals:* Fort Worth, TX: Harcourt Brace College.

Reksten, L. E. (2000). *Using technology to increase student learning.* Thousand Oaks, CA: Corwin Press.

Schlechty, P. C. (2001). *Shaking up the school house.* San Francisco: Jossey-Bass.

Sergiovanni, T. J. (1996) Leadership for the schoolhouse: How is it different? Why is it important? San Francisco: Jossey-Bass.

Sergiovanni, T. J. (2000). *The lifeworld of leadership: Creating culture, community, and personal meaning in our schools.* San Francisco: Jossey-Bass.

Sergiovanni, T. J., & Starratt, R. J. (1998). *Supervision: A redefinition* (6th ed.). Boston: McGraw-Hill.

Showers, B., & Joyce, B. (2002). *Student achievement through staff development.* (3rd ed.). Alexandria, VA: Association for Supervision & Curriculum Development.

Solomon, P. G. (2002). *The assessment bridge: Positive ways to link tests to learning, standards, and curriculum improvement.* Thousand Oaks, CA: Corwin Press.

Sunderman, G. L., Kim, J. S., & Orfield, G. (2005). *NCLB meets school realities: Lessons from the field.* Thousand Oaks, CA: Corwin Press.

Thompson, S. J., Quenemoen, R. F., Thurlow, M. L., & Ysseldyke, J. E. (2001). *Alternate assessments for students with disabilities.* Thousand Oaks, CA: Corwin Press.

Thurlow, M. L., Elliott, J. L., & Ysseldyke, J. E. (2002). *Testing students with disabilities: Practical strategies for complying with district and state requirements* (2nd ed.). Thousand Oaks, CA: Corwin Press.

Tomlinson, C. A. (1999). *The differentiated classroom: Responding to the needs of all learners.* Alexandria, VA: Association for Supervision & Curriculum Development.

Tomlinson, C. A. (2001). *How to differentiate instruction in mixed-ability classrooms* (2nd ed.). Alexandria, VA: Association for Supervision & Curriculum Development.

Tomlinson, C. A., & Allan, S. D. (2000). *Leadership for differentiating schools and classrooms.* Alexandria, VA: Association for Supervision & Curriculum Development.

Weil, J., Weil B., & Weil, M. (1998). *Models of teaching* (6th ed.). Needham Neights, MA: Simon and Schuster.

Whitaker, T. (1999). *Dealing with difficult teachers.* Larchmont, NY: Eye on Education.

Wilmore, E. L. (2004). *Principal induction: A standards-based model for administrator development.* Thousand Oaks, CA: Corwin Press.

Wilmore, E. L. (2007). *Teacher leadership: Improving teaching and learning from inside the classroom.* Thousand Oaks, CA: Corwin Press.

Wolfe, P. (2001). *Brain matters: Translating research into classroom practice.* Alexandria, VA: Association for Supervision & Curriculum Development.

Woodward, J., & Cuban, L. (Eds.). (2001). *Technology, curriculum, and professional development: Adapting schools to meet the needs of students with disabilities.* Thousand Oaks, CA: Corwin Press.

Worthen, B., Sanders, J., & Fitzpatrick, J. (1996). *Program evaluation, alternative approaches and practical guidelines* (2nd ed.). New York: Addison-Wesley.

Standard 3

Anderson, J. W. (2001). *The answers to questions that teachers most frequently ask.* Thousand Oaks, CA: Corwin Press.

Bennis, W. (1997). *Managing people is like herding cats.* Provo, UT: Executive Excellence.

Bjork, L. G., & Kowalski, T. J. (2005). *The contemporary superintendent: Preparation, practice, and development.* Thousand Oaks, CA: Corwin Press.

Brewer, E. W., & Achilles, C. M. (2008). *Finding funding: Grantwriting from start to finish, including project management and Internet use* (5th ed.). Thousand Oaks, CA: Corwin Press.

Burrup, P. E., Brimpley, V., Jr., & Garfield, R. R. (1998). *Financing education in a climate of change* (7th ed.). Boston: Allyn & Bacon.

Bush, T., & Middlewood, D. (2005). *Leading and managing people in education.* Thousand Oaks, CA: Sage.

Coleman, M., & Anderson, L. (Eds.). (2000). *Managing finance and resources in education.* London: Paul Chapman Educational Publishing.

Collinson, V., & Cook, T. F. (2006). *Organizational learning: Improving learning, teaching, and leading in school systems.* Thousand Oaks, CA: Sage.

Covey, S. R. (1990). *The seven habits of highly effective people.* New York: Simon & Schuster.

Di Giulio, R. C. (2001). *Educate, medicate, or litigate? What teachers, parents, and administrators must do about student behavior.* Thousand Oaks, CA: Corwin Press.

Dunklee, D. R., & Shoop, R. J. (2006). *The principal's quick-reference guide to school law: Reducing liability, litigation, and other potential legal tangles* (2nd ed.). Thousand Oaks, CA: Corwin Press.

Erlandson, D. A., Stark, P. L., & Ward, S. M. (1996). *Organizational oversight: Planning and scheduling for effectiveness.* Larchmont, NY: Eye on Education.

Fishbaugh, M. S. E., Schroth, G., & Berkeley, T. R. (Eds.). (2002). *Ensuring safe school environments: Exploring issues . . . seeking solutions.* Mahwah, NJ: Lawrence Erlbaum Associates.

Fitzwater, I. (1996). *Time management for school administrators.* Rockport, MA: Pro>Active.

Fullan, M. (2005). *Leadership sustainability: System thinkers in action.* Thousand Oaks, CA: Corwin Press.

Hoyle, J. R., Bjork, L. G., Collier, V., & Glass, T. (2005). *The superintendent as CEO: Standards-based performance.* Thousand Oaks, Corwin Press.

Knowles, C. (2002). *The first-time grantwriter's guide to success.* Thousand Oaks, CA: Corwin Press.

Ledeen, M. A. (1999). *Machiavelli on modern leadership.* New York: St. Martin's Press.

Levenson, S. (2006). *Big-time fundraising for today's schools.* Thousand Oaks, CA: Corwin Press.

Lunenburg, F. C., & Ornstein, A. C. (2000). *Educational administration: Concepts and practices* (3rd ed.). Belmont, CA: Wadsworth/Thomas Learning.

Marazza, L. L. (2003). *The five essentials of organizational excellence: Maximizing school-wide student achievement and performance.* Thousand Oaks, CA: Corwin Press.

McNamara, J. F., Erlandson, D. A., & McNamara, M. (1999). *Measurement and evaluation: Strategies for school improvement.* Larchmont, NY: Eye on Education.

Odden, A., & Archibald, S. (2001). *Reallocating resources: How to boost student achievement without asking for more.* Thousand Oaks, CA: Corwin Press.

Odden, A., & Kelley, C. (2002). *Paying teachers for what they know and do: New and smarter compensation strategies to improve schools* (2nd ed.). Thousand Oaks, CA: Corwin Press.

Parsons, B. A. (2001). *Evaluative inquiry: Using evaluation to promote student success.* Thousand Oaks, CA: Corwin Press.

Peterson, S. (2001). *The grantwriter's Internet companion: A resource for educators and others seeking grants and funding.* Thousand Oaks, CA: Corwin Press.

Ramsey, R. D. (2001). *Fiscal fitness for school administrators: How to stretch resources and do even more with less.* Thousand Oaks, CA: Corwin Press.

Sanders, J. R., & Sullins, C. D. (2005). *Evaluating school programs: An educator's guide* (3rd ed.). Thousand Oaks, CA: Corwin Press.

Sergiovanni, T. J. (2000). *The lifeworld of leadership.* San Francisco: Jossey-Bass.

Shoop, R. J., & Dunklee, D. R. (2006). *Anatomy of a lawsuit: What every education leader should know about legal actions.* Thousand Oaks, CA: Corwin Press.

Slavin, R. E., & Fashola, O. S. (1998). *Show me the evidence! Proven and promising programs for America's schools.* Thousand Oaks, CA: Corwin Press.

Smith, H. W. (1994). *The 10 natural laws of successful time and life management.* New York: Warner Books.

Sorenson, R. D., & Goldsmith, L. M. (2006). *The principal's guide to school budgeting.* Thousand Oaks, CA: Corwin Press.

Thomson, S. (Ed.). (1993). *Principals of our changing schools: Knowledge and skill base.* Alexandria, VA: National Policy Board for Educational Administration.

Van Geel, T., & Imber, M. *Education law* (2nd ed.). Mahwah, NJ: Lawrence Erlbaum Associates.

Standard 4

Batey, C. S. (1996). *Parents are lifesavers: A handbook for parent involvement in schools.* Thousand Oaks, CA: Corwin Press.

Beaudoin, M.-N., & Taylor, M. (2004). *Creating a positive school culture: How principals and teachers can solve problems together.* Thousand Oaks, CA: Corwin Press.

Bennis, W. (1999). *Old dogs, new tricks.* Provo, UT: Executive Excellence.

benShea, N. (2000). *What every principal would like to say . . . and what to say next time.* Thousand Oaks, CA: Corwin Press.

Burke, M. A., & Picus, L. O. (2001). *Developing community-empowered schools.* Thousand Oaks, CA: Corwin Press.

Chadwick, K. G. (2004). *Improving schools through community engagement: A practical guide for educators.* Thousand Oaks, CA: Corwin Press.

Decker, R. H. (1997). *When a crisis hits: Will your school be ready?* Thousand Oaks, CA: Corwin Press.

De Pree, M. (1997). *Leading without power: Finding hope in serving community.* San Francisco: Jossey-Bass.

Doyle, D. P., & Pimentel, S. (1999). *Raising the standard: An eight-step action guide for schools and communities* (2nd ed.). Thousand Oaks, CA: Corwin Press.

Drucker Foundation. (1996). *The leader of the future.* San Francisco: Jossey-Bass.

Duncan, S. F., & Goddard, H. W. (2005). *Family life education: Principles and practices for effective outreach.* Thousand Oaks, CA: Sage.

Epstein, J. L., Sanders, M. G., Simon, B. S. Salinas, K. C., Jansorn, N. R., & Van Voorhis, F. L. (2002). *School, family, and community partnerships: Your handbook for action* (2nd ed.). Thousand Oaks, CA: Corwin Press.

Veale J. R., Morley, R. E., & Erickson, C. L. (2002). *Practical evaluations for collaborative services: Goals, processes, tools, and reporting systems for school-based programs.* Thousand Oaks, CA: Corwin Press.

Giancola, J. M., & Hutchinson, J. K. (2005). *Transforming the culture of school leadership: Humanizing our practice.* Thousand Oaks, CA: Corwin Press.

Glaser, J. (2005). *Leading through collaboration: Guiding groups to productive solutions.* Thousand Oaks, CA: Corwin Press.

Harris, S. (2005). *Bravo teacher! Building relationships with actions that value others.* Larachmont, NY: Eye on Education.

Holcomb, E. L. (2001). *Asking the right questions: Techniques for collaboration and school change* (2nd ed.). Thousand Oaks, CA: Corwin Press.

Israel, S. E., Sisk, D. A., & Block, C. C. (2006). *Collaborative literacy: Using gifted strategies to enrich learning for every student.* Thousand Oaks, CA: Corwin Press.

Jayanthi, M., & Nelson, J. S. (2001). *Savvy decision making: An administrator's guide to using focus groups in schools.* Thousand Oaks, CA: Corwin Press.

Kaser, J., Mundry, S., Stiles, K. E., & Loucks-Horsley, S. (2006). *Leading every day: 124 actions for effective leadership* (2nd ed.). Thousand Oaks, CA: Corwin Press.

Kosmoski, G. J., & Pollack, D. R. (2006). *Managing difficult, frustrating, and hostile conversations: Strategies for savvy administrators* (2nd ed.). Thousand Oaks, CA: Corwin Press.

Longworth, N. (2006). *Learning cities, learning regions, learning communities: Lifelong learning and local government.* Florence, KY: Routledge.

McEwan, E. K. (1997). *Leading your team to excellence: How to make quality decisions.* Thousand Oaks, CA: Corwin Press.

Roberts, S. M., & Pruitt, E. Z. (2003). *Schools as professional learning communities: Collaborative activities and strategies for professional development.* Thousand Oaks, CA: Corwin Press.

Rubin, H. (2002). *Collaborative leadership: Developing effective partnerships in communities and schools.* Thousand Oaks, CA: Corwin Press.

Sanders, M. G. (2006). *Building school-community partnerships: Collaboration for student success.* Thousand Oaks, CA: Corwin Press.

Seiler, T. L. (2001). *Developing your case for support.* San Francisco: Jossey-Bass.

Sergiovanni, T. J. (1994). *Building community in schools.* San Francisco: Jossey-Bass.

Sullivan, S., & Glanz, J. (2005) *Building effective learning communities: Strategies for leadership, learning, & collaboration.* Thousand Oaks, CA: Corwin Press.

Thomas, S. J. (1999). *Designing surveys that work! A step-by-step guide.* Thousand Oaks, CA: Corwin Press.

Trump, K. S. (1998). *Practical school security: Basic guidelines for safe and secure schools.* Thousand Oaks, CA: Corwin Press.

Veale, J. R., Morley, R. E., & Erickson, C. L. (2001). *Practical evaluation for collaborative services: Goals, processes, tools, and reporting systems for school-based programs.* Thousand Oaks, CA: Corwin Press.

Wachter, J. C. (1999). *Classroom volunteers: Uh-oh! Or right on!* Thousand Oaks, CA: Corwin Press.

Weiss, H. B., Kreider, H. M., Labez, M. E., & Chatman, C. M. (Eds.). (2005). *Preparing educators to involve families: From theory to practice.* Thousand Oaks, CA: Sage.

Whitaker, T., Whitaker, B., & Lumpa, D. (2000). *Motivating and inspiring teachers: The educational leader's guide for building staff morale.* Larchmont, NY: Eye on Education.

Standard 5

Blanchard, K., Oncken, W., Jr., & Burrows, H. (1989). *The one minute manager meets the monkey.* New York: William Morrow.

Blanchard, K., & Peale, N. V. (1988). *The power of ethical management.* New York: Fawcett Columbine.

Blanchard, K., Zigarmi, P., & Zigmari, D. (1985). *Leadership and the one minute manager.* New York: William Morrow.

Brubaker, D. L. (2005). *The charismatic leader: The presentation of self and the creation of educational settings.* Thousand Oaks, CA: Corwin Press.

Cherry, D., & Spiegel, J. M. (2006). *Leadership, myth, & metaphor: Finding common ground to guide effective school change.* Thousand Oaks, CA: Corwin Press.

Dunklee, D. R. (2000). *If you want to lead, not just manage: A primer for principals.* Thousand Oaks, CA: Corwin Press.

Dunklee, D. R., & Shoop, R. J. (2006). *The principal's quick-reference guide to school law: Reducing liability, litigation, and other potential legal tangles* (2nd ed.). Thousand Oaks: Corwin Press.

Feinberg, W. (2006). *For goodness sake: Religious schools and education for democratic citizenry.* Florence, KY: Routledge.

Fullan, M. (2003). *The moral imperative of school leadership.* Thousand Oaks, CA: Corwin Press.

Gray, K. C. (1999). *Getting real: Helping teens find their future.* Thousand Oaks, CA: Corwin Press.

Halstead, J. M., & Pike, M. *Citizenship and moral education: Values in action.* Florence, KY: Routledge.

Houston, P. D., & Sokolow, S. L. (2006). *The spiritual dimension of leadership: 8 key principles to leading more effectively.* Thousand Oaks, CA: Corwin Press.

Hoyle, J. R. (2002). *Leadership and the force of love: Six keys to motivating with love.* Thousand Oaks, CA: Corwin Press.

Josephson, M. S., & Hanson, W. (1998). *The power of character.* San Francisco: Jossey-Bass.

Kochanek, J. R. (2005). *Building trust for better schools: Research-based practices.* Thousand Oaks, CA: Corwin Press.

Miller, J. P. (2006). *Educating for wisdom and compassion: Creating conditions for timeless learning.* Thousand Oaks, CA: Corwin Press.

Osier, J. L., & Fox, H. P. (2001). *Settle conflicts right now! A step-by-step guide for K–6 classrooms.* Thousand Oaks, CA: Corwin Press.

Osterman, K. F., & Kottkamp, R. B. (2004). *Reflective practice for educators: Professional development to improve student learning* (2nd ed.). Thousand Oaks, CA: Corwin Press.

Pellicer, L.O. (1999). *Caring enough to lead: Schools and the sacred trust.* Thousand Oaks, CA: Corwin Press.

Pellicer, L. O. (2007). *Caring enough to lead: How reflective practice leads to moral leadership* (3rd ed.). Thousand Oaks, CA: Corwin Press.

Podesta, C. (with Sanderson, V.). (1999). *Life would be easy if it weren't for other people.* Thousand Oaks, CA: Corwin Press.

Podesta, C. (2001). *Self-esteem and the 6-second secret* (updated ed.). Thousand Oaks, CA: Corwin Press.

Pryor, B. W., & Pryor, C. R. (2005). *The school leader's guide to understanding attitude and influencing behavior: Working with teachers, parents, students, and the community.* Thousand Oaks, CA: Corwin Press.

Reagan, T. G., Case, C. W., & Brubacher, J. W. (2000). *Becoming a reflective educator: How to build a culture of inquiry in the schools* (2nd ed.). Thousand Oaks, CA: Corwin Press.

Sergiovanni, T. J. (1992). *Moral leadership: Getting to the heart of school improvement.* San Francisco: Jossey-Bass.

Snowden, P. E., & Gorton, R. A. (1998). *School leadership and administration: Important concepts, case studies, and simulations* (5th ed.). New York: McGraw-Hill.

Strike, K. A. (2006). *Ethical leadership in schools: Creating community in an environment of accountability.* Thousand Oaks, CA: Corwin Press.

Taulbert, C. L. (2006). *Eight habits of the heart for educators: Building strong school communities through timeless values.* Thousand Oaks, CA: Corwin Press.

York-Barr, J., Sommers, W. A., Ghere, G. S., & Montie, J. (2006). *Reflective practice to improve schools: An action guide for educators* (2nd ed.). Thousand Oaks, CA: Corwin Press.

Standard 6

Bates, D., Durka, G., & Schweitzer, F. (2005). *Education, religion and society: Essays in honour of John M. Hull.* Florence, KY: Routledge.

Bell, L., & Stevenson, H. (2006). *Education policy: Process, themes and impact.* Florence, KY: Routledge.

Covey, S. R. (1990). *Principle-centered leadership.* New York: Simon & Schuster.

Covey, S. R., Merrill, A. R., & Merrill, R. R. (1994). *First things first.* New York: Simon & Schuster.

English, F. W. (1994). *Theory in educational administration.* New York: HarperCollins.

Fiore, D. J., & Whitaker, T. (2001). *Dealing with difficult parents (and with parents in difficult situations).* Larchmont, NY: Eye on Education.

Hoy, W. H., & Miskel, C. G. (1996). *Educational administration: Theory, research, and practice* (5th ed.). New York: McGraw-Hill.

Kosmoski, G. J., & Pollack, D. R. (2005). *Managing difficult, frustrating, and hostile conversations* (2nd ed.). Thousand Oaks, CA: Corwin Press.

Leithwood, K. (Ed.). (1995). *Effective school district leadership: Transforming politics into education.* Albany: State University of New York Press.

McEwan, E. K. (2005). *How to deal with parents who are angry, troubled, afraid, or just plain crazy* (2nd ed.). Thousand Oaks, CA: Corwin Press.

Olssen, M., Codd, J. A., & O'Neill, A. M. (2004). *Education policy: Globalization, citizenship and democracy.* Thousand Oaks, CA: Sage.

Palestini, R. H. (1999). *Educational administration: Leading with mind and heart.* Lancaster, PA: Technomic.

Reinhartz, J., & Beach, D. M. (2001). *Foundations of educational leadership: Changing schools, changing roles.* Boston: Allyn & Bacon.

Schmieder, J. H., & Cairns, D. (1996). *Ten skills of highly effective principals.* Lancaster, PA: Technomic.

Schumaker, D. R., & Sommers, W. A. (2001). *Being a successful principal: Riding the wave of change without drowning.* Thousand Oaks, CA: Corwin Press.

Skrla, L., Erlandson, D. A., Reed, E. M., & Wilson, A. P. (2001). *The emerging principalship.* Larchmont, NY: Eye on Education.

Smith, M. L., Miller-Kahn, L., Heinecke, W., & Jarvis, P. F. (2003). *Political spectacle and the fate of American schools.* Florence, KY: Routledge.

Sperry, D. J. (1999). *Working in a legal and regulatory environment: A handbook for school leaders.* Larchmont, NY: Eye on Education.

Streshly, W. A., Walsh, J., & Frase, L. E. (2001). *Avoiding legal hassles: What school administrators really need to know* (2nd ed.). Thousand Oaks, CA: Corwin Press.

Strike, K. A. (2006). *Ethical leadership in schools: Creating community in an environment of accountability.* Thousand Oaks, CA: Corwin Press.

Townsend, R. S., Johnston, G. L., Gross, G. E., Lynch, P., Garcy, L. Roberts, B., & Novotney, P. B. (2006). *Effective superintendent-school board practices: Strategies for developing and maintaining a good relationship with your board.* Thousand Oaks, CA: Corwin Press.

Standard 7

Alvy, H. B., & Robbins, P. (1998). *If I only knew . . . Success strategies for navigating the principalship.* Thousand Oaks, CA: Corwin Press.

benShea, N. (2006). *The journey to greatness: And how to get there!* Thousand Oaks, CA: Corwin Press.

Bjork, L. G., & Kowalski, T. J. (Eds.). (2005). *The contemporary superintendent: Preparation, practice, and development.* Thousand Oaks, CA: Corwin Press.

Briggs, A., Busher, H., & Sage, R. (2006). *Leading learning: International perspectives.* Florence, KY: Routledge.

Brown, G., & Irby, B. J. (2001). *The principal portfolio* (2nd ed.). Thousand Oaks, CA: Corwin Press.

Cambron-McCabe, N., Cunningham, L. L., Harvey, J., & Koff, R. H. (2005). *The superintendent's field book: A guide for leaders of learning.* Thousand Oaks, CA: Corwin Press.

Capasso, R. L., & Daresh, J. C. (2001). *The school administrator internship handbook: Leading, mentoring, and participating in the internship program.* Thousand Oaks, CA: Corwin Press.

Daresh, J. (2001). *What it means to be a principal: Your guide to leadership.* Thousand Oaks, CA: Corwin Press.

Daresh, J. (2006). *Beginning the principalship: A practical guide for new school leaders* (3rd ed.). Thousand Oaks, CA: Corwin Press.

Green, H. (2004). *Professional standards for teachers and school leaders: A key to school improvement.* Florence, KY: Routledge.

Hartzell, G. N., Williams, R. C., & Nelson, K. T. (1995). *New voices in the field: The work lives of first-year assistant principals.* Thousand Oaks, CA: Corwin Press.

Irby, B. J., & Brown, G. (2000). *The career advancement portfolio.* Thousand Oaks, CA: Corwin Press.

Jarvis, P. (2007). *Lifelong learning and the learning society: Requirements and provision.* Florence, KY: Routledge.

Johnson, R. S., Mims-Cox, J. S., & Doyle-Nichols, A. (2006). *Developing portfolios in education: A guide to reflection, inquiry, and assessment.* Thousand Oaks, CA: Sage.

Kowalski, T. J. (2005). *The school superintendent: Theory, practice, and cases* (2nd ed.). Thousand Oaks, CA: Sage.

McCabe, N., Cunningham, L. L., Harvey, J., & Koff, R. H. (2005). *The superintendent's fieldbook: A guide for leaders of learning.* Thousand Oaks, CA: Corwin.

Metzger, C. (2006). *Balancing leadership and personal growth: The school administrator's guide.* Thousand Oaks, CA: Corwin Press.

Montgomery, K., & Wiley, D. (2008) *Building e-portfolios using PowerPoint: A guide for educators* (2nd ed.). Thousand Oaks, CA: Sage.

Nicoll, K. (2006). *Flexibility and lifelong learning: Policy, discourse, politics.* Florence, KY: Routledge.

Nicholls, G. (2005). *The challenge to scholarship: Rethinking learning, teaching and research.* Florence, KY: Routledge.

Reiss, K. (2006). *Leadership coaching for educators: Bringing out the best in school administrators.* Thousand Oaks, CA: Corwin Press.

Robbins, P., & Alvy, H. B. (2003). *The principal's companion: Strategies and hints to make the job easier* (2nd ed.). Thousand Oaks, CA: Corwin Press.

Robinson, V., & Lai, M. K. (2006). *Practitioner research for educators: A guide to improving classrooms and schools.* Thousand Oaks, CA: Corwin Press.

Sharp, W. L., Walter, J. K., & Sharp, H. M. (1998). *Case studies for school leaders: Implementing the ISLLC standards.* Lancaster, PA: Technomic.

Villani, S. (1999). *Are you sure you're the principal? On being an authentic leader.* Thousand Oaks, CA: Corwin Press.

Wilmore, E. L. (2002). *Principal leadership: Applying the new Educational Leadership Constituent Council (ELCC) standards.* Thousand Oaks, CA: Corwin Press.

Wyatt, R. L., III, & Looper, S. (2004). *So you have to have a portfolio: A teacher's guide to preparation and presentation* (2nd ed.). Thousand Oaks, CA: Corwin Press.

References

Beaudoin, M. N., & Taylor, M. (2004). *Creating a positive school culture: How principals and teachers can solve problems together.* Thousand Oaks, CA: Corwin Press.

Berman, S. (2005, November). Restoring progressive values. *School Administrator, 62*(10), 16.

Björk, L. G., & Keedy, J. L. (Eds.). (2003). Superintendent shortage: Myth and reality [Special issue]. *Journal of School Leadership, 13*(3/4).

Björk, L. G., & Kowalski, T. J. (2005). *The contemporary superintendent: Preparation, practice, and development.* Thousand Oaks, CA: Sage Publications.

Bolman, L. G., & Deal, T. E. (1997). *Reframing organizations: Artistry, choice and leadership* (2nd ed.). San Francisco: Jossey-Bass.

Bolman, L. G., & Deal, T. E. (2006). *The wizard and the warrior: Leading with passion and power.* San Francisco: Jossey-Bass.

Bowler, M. (2000, May 14). Shrinking talent pool hampers hunt for school superintendents. *Houston Chronicle,* p. 19.

Cambron-McCabe, N. (2005). *The superintendent's field book.* Thousand Oaks, CA: Corwin Press.

Carter, D., Glass, T. E., & Hord, S. (Eds.). (1993). *Selecting, preparing, and developing the school district superintendent.* Washington, DC: Falmer Press.

Christopher, G. (2007). The value of partnerships. *American School Board Journal, 194*(1), 42–43.

Clason, G. (1955). *The richest man in Babylon.* New York: Signet.

Czaja, M., & Harman, M. J. (1997, December 20). Excessive school district turnover: An explorative study in Texas. *International Electronic Journal for Leadership in Learning, 1*(6). Retrieved December 14, 2006, from www.ucalgary.ca/~iejll/volume1/CzajaHarmanv1n6.html

Deal, T. E., & Bolman, L. G. (2001). *Leading with soul.* San Francisco: Jossey-Bass.

Dillon, N., & Vail, K. (2005). 8 districts to watch. *American School Board Journal, 192*(9), 22–25.

Fenwick, L. T. (2000). Few lame ducks or placeholders: A study of the interim ranks. *School Administrator, 57*(3), 33–34.

Fryer, B., & Gardner, H. (2007, March). The ethical mind: A conversation with psychologist Howard Gardner. *Harvard Business Review, 85,* 51–56.

Fullan, M. (2001). *Leading in a culture of change.* San Francisco: Jossey-Bass.

Fullan, M. (2003). *The moral imperative of school leadership.* Thousand Oaks, CA: Corwin Press.

Fullan, M. (2005). *Leadership & sustainability: System thinkers in action.* Thousand Oaks, CA: Corwin Press.

Fusarelli, B. C., & Fusarelli, L. D. (2005). Reconceptualizing the superintendency: Superintendents as applied social scientists and social activists. In L. G. Björk & T. J. Kowalski (Eds.), *The contemporary superintendent: Preparation, practice, and development* (pp. 187–206). Thousand Oaks, CA: Corwin Press.

Glatter, R. (1996). *School administration: Persistent dilemmas in preparation and practice.* Westport, CT: Praeger.

Greenleaf, R. (1982). *Servant as leader.* Westfield, IN: Robert Greenleaf Center.

Greenleaf, R. K. (1991). *Servant leadership: A journey into the nature of legitimate power and greatness.* New York: Paulist Press.

Henry, T. (2000, January 26). Superintendents in demand. *USA Today,* A1.

Hoyle, J. (2004). *Superintendent as CEO.* Thousand Oaks, CA: Corwin Press.

Hoyle, J. (2006). *Leadership and futuring: Making visions happen.* Thousand Oaks, CA: Corwin.

Hoyle, J. R., Bjork, L. G., Collier, V., & Glass, T. (2005). *The superintendent as CEO: Standards-based performance.* Thousand Oaks, CA: Corwin Press.

Kelley, R., Starr, M., & Conant, E. (2007, April 23). A team stands tall. *Newsweek, 149,* 32.

Krantz, C. (2000, March 3). More women hold top school jobs: Women make inroads in Iowa schools. *Des Moines Register,* p. 1.

Leithwood, K. (Ed.). (1995). *Effective school leadership: Transforming politics into education.* Albany: State University of New York Press.

Natt, J. G. (2000, January 27). Superintendents see shortage of applicants for top spots as a 'Serious Crisis.' *AASA Leadership News.* Retrieved January 22, 2007, from www.aasa.org/career/content.cfm?ItemNumber=2296

Pascopella, A. (2004). Community connections. *District Administration, 40*(6), 32–37.

Payne, R. K. (2005). *A framework for understanding poverty.* Highlands, TX: Aha! Process, Inc.

Payne, R. K. (2006). *Discipline strategies for the classroom: Working with students.* Highlands, TX: Aha! Process, Inc.

Pellicer, L. O. (2003). *Caring enough to lead: How reflective thought leads to moral leadership.* Thousand Oaks, CA: Corwin Press.

Sanders, N. M., & Simpson, J., (2006). *State policy framework to develop highly qualified administrators.* Washington, DC: Council of Chief State School Officers (CCSSO).

Schlechty, P. C. (2001). *Shaking up the school house: How to support and sustain educational innovation.* San Francisco: Jossey-Bass.

Schlechty, P. C. (2005). *Creating great schools: Six critical systems at the heart of educational innovation.* San Francisco: Jossey-Bass.

Sergiovanni, T. J. (1990). *Value-added leadership: How to get extraordinary performance in schools.* Orlando, FL: Harcourt Brace Jovanovich.

Sergiovanni, T. J. (1992). *Moral leadership: Getting to the heart of school improvement.* San Francisco: Jossey-Bass.

Sergiovanni, T. J. (1994). *Building community in schools.* San Francisco: Jossey-Bass.

Sergiovanni, T. J. (1996) *Leadership for the schoolhouse: How is it different? Why is it important?* San Francisco: Jossey-Bass.

Sergiovanni, T. J. (2000). *The lifeworld of leadership: Creating culture, community, and personal meaning in our schools.* San Francisco: Jossey-Bass.

Sergiovanni, T. J. (2001). *The principalship: A reflective practice perspective* (4th ed.). Needham Heights, MA: Allyn and Bacon.

Standards for Advanced Programs in Educational Leadership for Principals, Superintendents, Curriculum Directors, and Supervisors. (2002). Washington, DC: National Policy Board for Educational Administration. Retrieved from www.npbea.org/ELCC/ELCCStandards%20_5–02.pdf

Strike, K. A. (2007). *Ethical leadership in schools.* Thousand Oaks, CA: Corwin Press.

Texas Education Code, 18 Tex. Stat. Ann. § 21.046 (Vernon, 2006).

Tingley, S. (1996, October 30). Pooling our resources: Why are there so few candidates for superintendent? Maybe we're looking in the wrong place. *Education Week, 16,* 38–48.

Townsen, R. S. (2007). *Effective superintendent-school board practices.* Thousand Oaks, CA: Corwin Press.

Wasserman, S. (2004). A city and school district united. *School Planning & Management, 43*(10), 30–32.

Wilmore, E. L. (2002). *Principal leadership: Applying the new Educational Leadership Constituent Council (ELCC) Standards.* Thousand Oaks, CA: Corwin Press.

Wilmore, E. L. (2004). *Principal induction: A standards-based model for administrator development.* Thousand Oaks, CA: Corwin Press.

Wilmore, E. L. (2007). *Teacher leadership: Improving teaching and learning from inside the classroom.* Thousand Oaks, CA: Corwin Press.

Texas Examinations of Educator Standards: Preparation Manual (Superintendent). (2006). Austin: Texas Education Agency. Retrieved from www.texes.ets.org/assets/pdf/testprep_manuals/064_superintendent_55069_web.pdf

Texas Examinations of Educator Standards: Preparation Manual (Superintendent: District Profile Packet). (2006). Austin: Texas Education Agency. Retrieved from www.texes.ets.org/assets/pdf/testprep_manuals/064_superintendent2.pdf

Index

CORWIN PRESS

The Corwin Press logo—a raven striding across an open book—represents the union of courage and learning. Corwin Press is committed to improving education for all learners by publishing books and other professional development resources for those serving the field of PreK–12 education. By providing practical, hands-on materials, Corwin Press continues to carry out the promise of its motto: **"Helping Educators Do Their Work Better."**